Praise for the Football School series

"Hilarious ... packed with amazing football facts, cartoons, jokes..."
The Week Junior

"Will spark a love of learning in any child who reads it...
Intelligent, inspiring, funny..."
Head of Education, Premier League

"We love this book series!"
Match of the Day Weekly

"A dream for young footie fans."
The Sun

"Funny, informative and hugely entertaining..."
BookTrust

To Aldyr – A.B.

To ABC, with love – B.L.

For my mum – S.G.

First published 2018 by Walker Books Ltd
87 Vauxhall Walk, London SE11 5HJ

This edition published 2019

2 4 6 8 10 9 7 5 3

This book has been typeset in Palatino

Printed and bound by CPI Group (UK) Ltd, Croydon CR0 4YY

British Library Cataloguing in Publication Data:
a catalogue record for this book is available from the British Library

ISBN 978-1-4063-8640-0

WALKER BOOKS

FSC www.fsc.org MIX Paper from responsible sources FSC® C020471

www.walker.co.uk

www.footballschool.co

FOOTBALL SCHOOL

Season 3

WHERE FOOTBALL ~~EXPLAINS~~ tackles THE WORLD

ALEX BELLOS & BEN LYTTLETON

Illustrated by Spike Gerrell

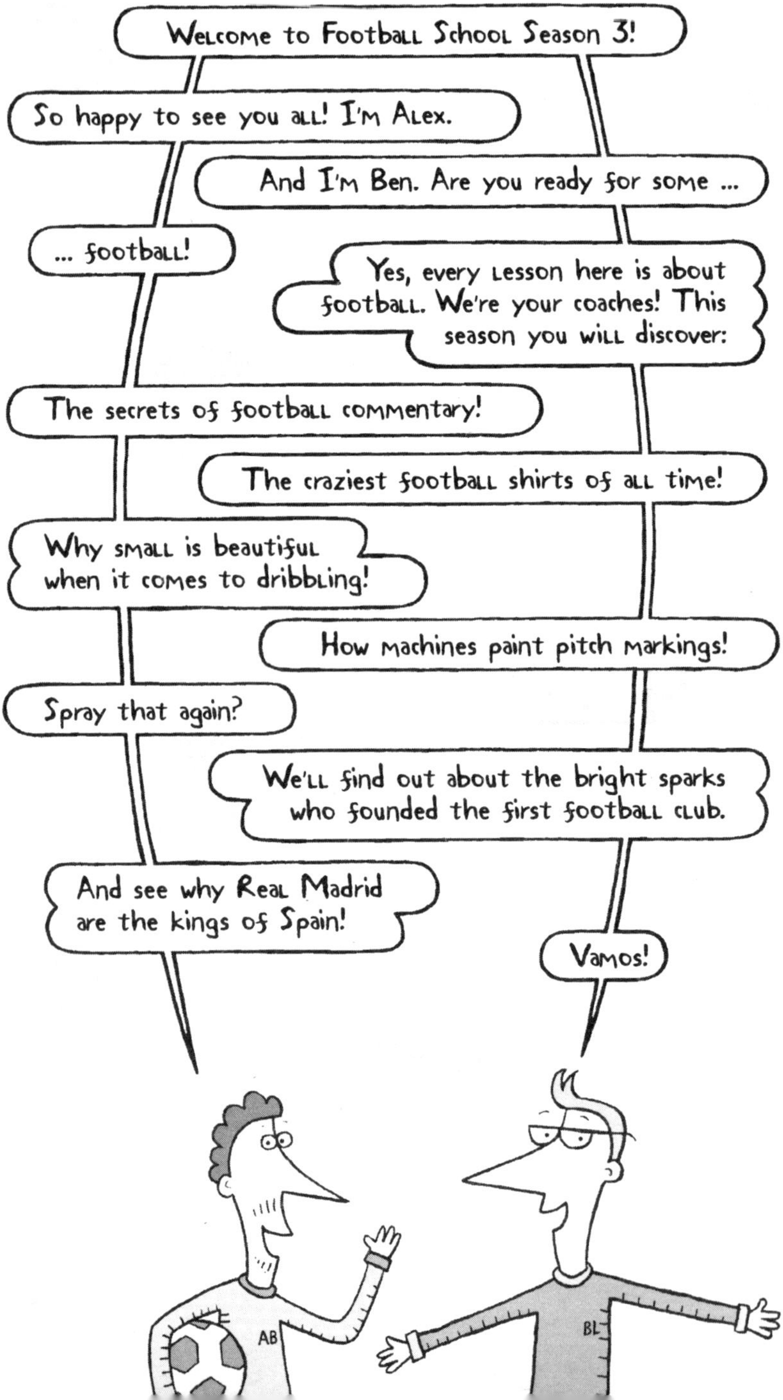
Welcome to Football School Season 3!
So happy to see you all! I'm Alex.
And I'm Ben. Are you ready for some ...
... football!
Yes, every lesson here is about football. We're your coaches! This season you will discover:
The secrets of football commentary!
The craziest football shirts of all time!
Why small is beautiful when it comes to dribbling!
How machines paint pitch markings!
Spray that again?
We'll find out about the bright sparks who founded the first football club.
And see why Real Madrid are the kings of Spain!
Vamos!
AB
BL

We've spoken to incredible experts...
Including the man who taught Cristiano Ronaldo how to sleep.
And the woman who teaches footballers how to cut their toenails.
We even interviewed a shiny, big-eared 100-year-old Scot!
This season we have something new: we're going on a school trip!
To learn about football, burping cows and farting bugs!
BURPPPP! PARRRPPP!
If you read this book, you will become a better footballer.
Definitely a smarter one.
And one with healthier feet!
AB
BL

MEET YOUR COACHES

ALEX "BELLINHOS" BELLOS

Coach Stats

Birthplace: Oxford
Birthday: 22 November
Favourite food: Pickled gherkins
Favourite word: Four (it is the only word that accurately describes the number of letters it has!)
Favourite ice-cream flavour: Chocolate
Favourite TV show: Any sports documentary
Favourite joke: Time flies like an arrow. Fruit flies like a banana
Number of footballs in house: 3
Three favourite forwards: Pelé, Marta, Lionel Messi
Favourite stadium visited: San Siro, Milan
Favourite freestyle move: Seal dribble
Preferred goal celebration: Brazilian samba dance

Coach Stats

Birthplace: London
Birthday: 18 September
Favourite food: Pizza
Favourite word: GOAAAALLL!
Favourite ice-cream flavour: Honeycomb
Favourite TV show: Match of the Day
Favourite joke: Alex's hair (not really!)
Number of footballs in house: 7
Three favourite forwards: Kylian Mbappé, Johan Cruyff, Nadia Nadim
Favourite stadium visited: Estádio Municipal de Braga, Portugal
Favourite freestyle move: Rainbow flick
Preferred goal celebration: Aeroplane

BEN "THE PEN" LYTTLETON

TIMETABLE

	MONDAY	TUESDAY
REGISTRATION		
LESSON 1	BIOLOGY 10–19	ZOOLOGY 46–59
LESSON 2		
LESSON 3	ENGLISH 20–33	POLITICS 60–71
LESSON 4		
LUNCH 1.00–2.00PM		
LESSON 5	PHYSICS 34–45	PSHE 72–83

Find the answers to the quizzes on page 174. But no cheating!
BL

Monday
Lesson 1+2

BIOLOGY

Professional footballers seem to glow. Their well-toned bodies and perfect posture are signs of fitness and well-being. They spend money on dentistry to make sure they have gleaming white teeth. On the top of their heads is always – always – a fashionable flourish of hair. They are a picture of good health, a sight to behold.

Just don't look at their feet!

Claw toes. Bruises. Blisters. Bunions. Calluses. Corns. Swellings. Verrucas. Eughhh! Footballers' feet are the victims of a lifetime of kicking a ball around for hours a day. And there's a lot that can go wrong with a foot if it is not looked after properly. Believe us – we've spoken to an expert!

To kick off Season 3 at Football School, we are going to look at our lowermost limb: those five-pronged platforms that bear the weight of our entire bodies, and whose name is contained in the first four letters of our favourite sport.

There's trouble afoot and we're not going to tiptoe around the details!

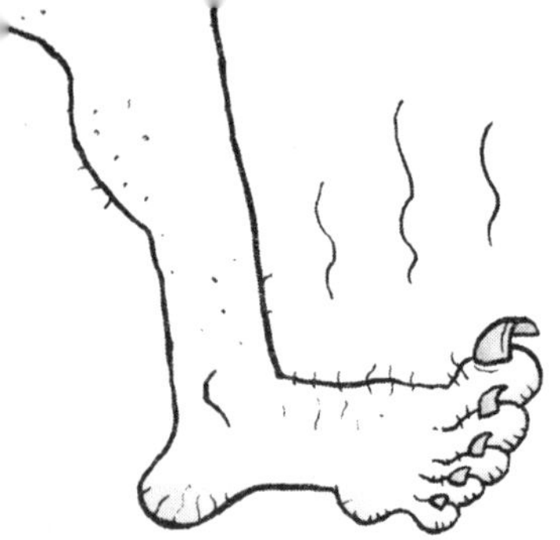

POD SPODS

A doctor who specializes in feet is called a **podiatrist**. Many clubs employ a podiatrist because it is so important that footballers keep their feet in good condition. Just as firefighters take care of their hoses, singers take care of their voices and illustrator Spike takes care of his pencils, footballers must look after their feet in order to do their jobs properly.

We spoke to Nutan Shah, one of the UK's top podiatrists, who has worked with many top clubs and the England team. She's peeled the socks off the subject in order to let us know the ugly truth about footballers' tootsies. "Not a pretty sight!" she revealed to us. "The feet get battered. A few players have immaculate feet but very few."

It pays to look after your paws. Shah says that a footballer's most valuable accessories are not their fancy sunglasses, a fast car or the latest phone, but a pair of nail clippers and a nail file. Badly looked after feet can mean players miss weeks of action.

Footballers are all too aware of their disfigured trotters, which is why Shah told us that at the end of the season they often ask her if she can make their feet look pretty. "They are about to go on holiday and they want their feet to look nice on the beach. Footballers are able to look after their hands and face throughout the season, but their feet are completely bashed about."

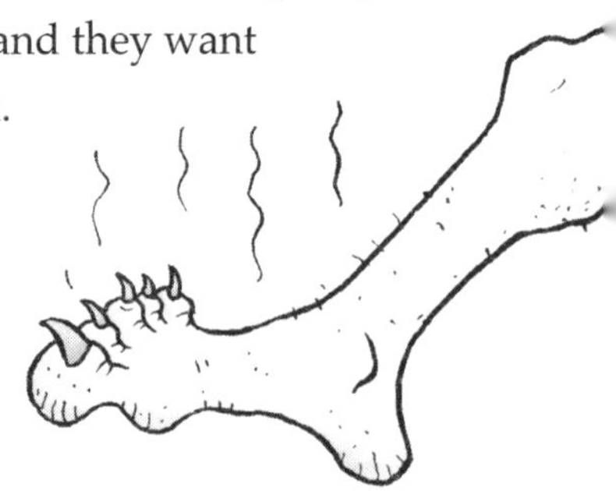

TIPS FOR TOES

When it comes to looking after your feet, the first thing to get right is the size of your shoe.

Footballers often wear boots that are too tight, maybe a size or a size and a half smaller than what their podiatrist recommends. Many footballers prefer tight boots because it makes them feel that the shoe is like a second skin, which gives them more control of the ball. But it creates foot problems down the line. It's a pressing issue!

Footballers also need to be very careful about what shoes they wear in their free time. Podiatrists see problems emerge when footballers wear stiff fashion shoes that rub their feet and give them calluses, blisters and even open sores called ulcers. If an athlete wants to protect their Achilles tendon, they need to wear shoes that have an incline in the heel, so flat shoes like Converse trainers or flip-flops are not recommended. Nor are stilettos!

Another major problem is moisture. This isn't just because footballers run around a lot, which gives them hot and sweaty feet. It's also because they spend so much time washing and soaking their feet in water. As part of their fitness and hygiene routines, footballers are often in the shower, Jacuzzi or bath. If the feet stay too wet then they are at risk of fungal infections, and if they dry out too much they get dry and cracked skin. A sensible footballer will rub moisturiser on their feet. Smooth!

Foot Complaints

athlete's foot • An itchy rash caused by a tiny fungus that eats dead skin. It got its name because the fungus thrives in moist, warm places like the damp surfaces in swimming pools and gyms where athletes spend their time. In order to avoid catching athlete's foot, it's advisable to wear flip-flops at the pool or gym.

black toe • If a player hits their toe hard – perhaps by kicking the ground by mistake, or another player treading on their feet – the skin underneath the nail can bleed, turning it black or purple. In certain cases of black toe, the entire nail will eventually fall off.

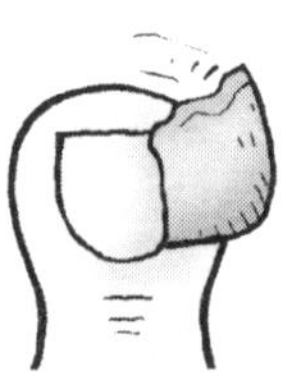

callus • A yellowy blob of hard skin, caused by something hard rubbing against the skin continuously for a long time. For example, the little lump many people get on their middle finger from where a pencil rubs when they write is a callus. Calluses tend to appear on the feet more than anywhere else, because whenever we walk or run our feet rub against the inside of our shoes. A small callus can help protect the foot, but once they get big they cause discomfort and have to be removed. Footballers and other sportspeople are susceptible to calluses, especially if their boots are too tight.

claw toe • A condition where all the toes, apart from the big toe, curl in, so rather than lying flat, they look like animal claws. Most footballers have claw toe, the result of wearing boots that have been too tight from a young age. If a footballer has claw toe, they are more likely to damage their toenails and get more calluses and corns.

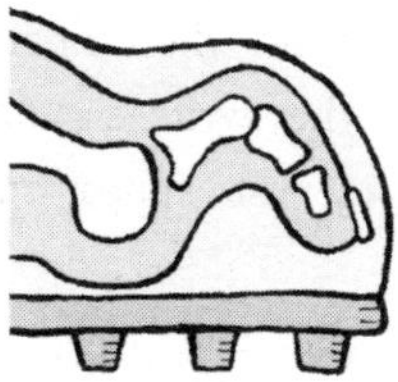

corn • A hard, circular callus on the toes which is caused by friction putting pressure on a single point. In some extreme cases, corns are filed down or sliced off with a knife.

ingrown toenail • When a toenail is not clipped properly there is the risk that it may start to grow into the skin. Ingrown toenails are not a silly little problem. They can cause huge pain and easily lead to a footballer having to take weeks out injured. To avoid them, a footballer should check their toenails every day, and file down any sharp bits that might dig into the skin.

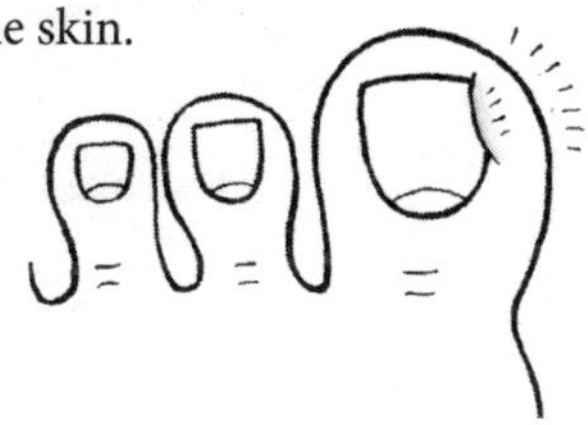

verruca • A wart that you get on the sole of your foot. Verrucas are contagious and can be spread through the watery floors of communal showers and swimming pools. Football clubs are obsessively vigilant for any players with verrucas, since if one person has them, they can quickly spread through a whole team. If you get a verruca and it causes pain, one treatment is for a doctor to freeze it so it falls off.

Foot Anatomy

The **anatomy** of a living thing is a description of its internal structure. Here's a glimpse into the anatomy of the foot – as you'll see, it's quite a *feet* of engineering!

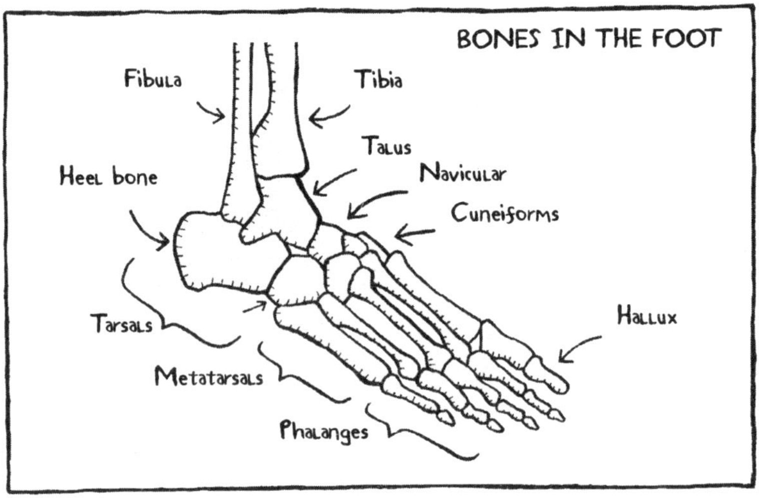

bones • Each foot contains 26 bones and 33 joints, meaning that about a quarter of all the bones in our body are in the feet. The only limbs in our body with a more complicated bone structure are our hands, but feet undergo much more physical stress than the hands because feet carry the entire weight of our body. The bones that are the most at risk of injury for footballers are the **metatarsals**, on the forefoot, since they are the thinnest in the foot and, unlike the **phalanges** in the toes, metatarsals cannot flex out of the way.

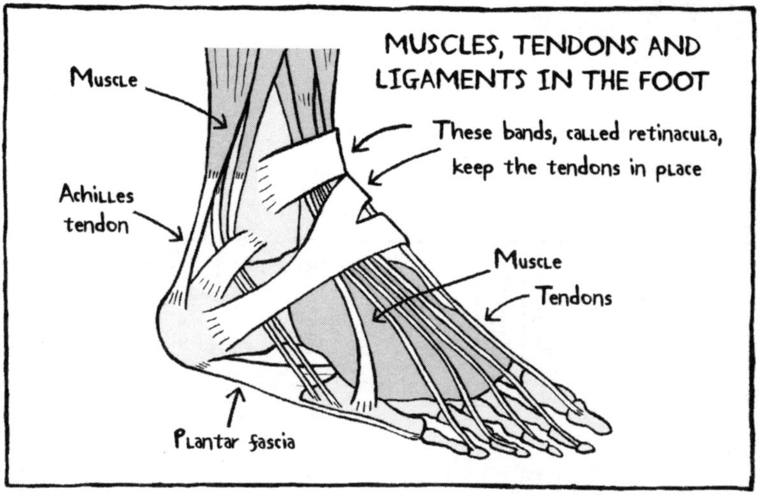

skin • The skin under the ball of your foot and under the heel is thicker than the skin anywhere else on your body. This is because there are extra layers of fat, a bit like bubble wrap, which act as shock absorbers when you walk. Comfy!

ligaments • Ligaments join bones to bones. An important ligament in the foot is the **plantar fascia**, which runs along the sole from the heel to the toes. When you step on your foot, the plantar fascia stretches like a spring, and when you lift the foot up, the ligament releases, which gives the foot a bounce of energy. It is literally a spring in your step!

tendons • Tendons join muscle to bone. The main tendon in the foot is the **Achilles tendon**, which joins the calf muscle to the heel. The Achilles tendon acts like a lever that pushes your foot away from the leg, which is what enables us to run, jump, walk up stairs and stand on tiptoe. Scientists have discovered that sprinters, on average, have shorter Achilles tendons than other people, because this gives them more force when pushing off the ground.

FOOT FROMAGE

Everyone with a nose knows that feet often infuse socks with a distinctive, cheesy aroma. You should smell Ben's after he's been for a run! This pongy perfume is the result of the fact that the soles of the feet (as well as the palms of the hand) have the highest density of sweat glands in the entire human body. Sweat on its own does not smell. But moist, warm socks provide the perfect habitat for **bacteria** that live on the skin to thrive. The bacteria eat dead skin and the process produces a smelly gas with a familiar cheesy scent. Scientists who study smelly socks discovered that the same malodorous bacteria in our feet are present in smelly cheeses, such as reeky Limburger, from Germany. Whiffy!

BIOLOGY QUIZ

1. What is the name of a doctor who specialises in treating feet?

a) Podiatrist
b) Sole man
c) Faith heeler
d) Head, shoulders, knees and toes surgeon

2. Former England striker Darius Vassell once missed three games due to injury because he did what to his toe, after it had become swollen?

a) He tried to clip off the nail, but cut a chunk out of his toe.
b) He peeled off the toenail by accident and it became too painful to put his boots on.
c) He drilled through his nail to drain the blood and ease the pressure, and the toe became infected.
d) He painted the toenail with varnish and became ill from inhaling the fumes.

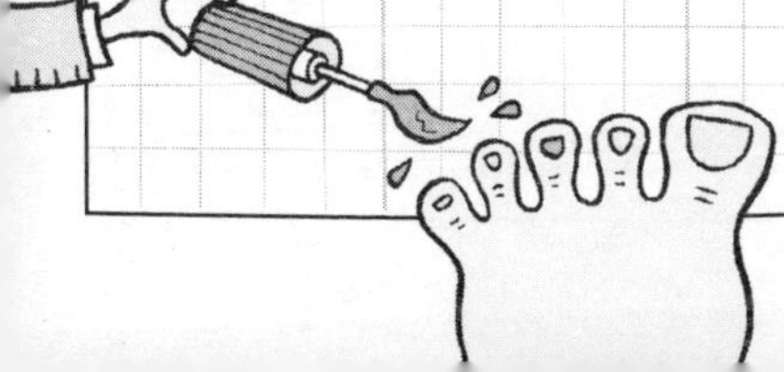

3. How did Achilles, the hero from Greek mythology, die, which is the reason why the tendon in our heel is named after him?

a) A lightning bolt hit him in the heel
b) A poisoned arrow hit him in the heel
c) A snake bit him on the heel
d) A football hit him on the heel

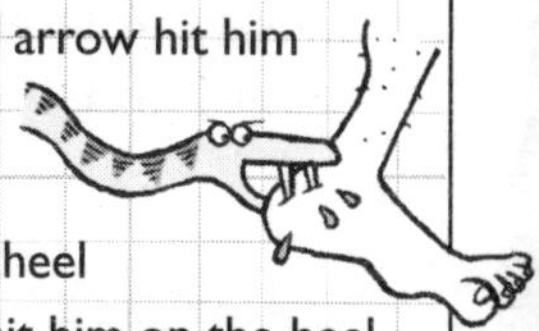

4. Which of the following players has the biggest feet?

a) Cristiano Ronaldo
b) David Silva
c) Paul Pogba
d) Romelu Lukaku

5. Which animal is attracted to the smell of sweaty socks?

a) Tiger
b) Skunk
c) Mosquito
d) Snail

Monday
Lesson 3+4

ENGLISH

Listen up! Do you like the sound of your own voice? Do you get told off for talking too much? Do you love words – and football? Would you like to talk about football for the rest of your life? Well, we might have the job for you! You'd have to travel a lot and have the gift of the gab. But you'd also get to watch all the drama of the biggest games unfold live in front of you. Too exciting for words!

In this lesson we are going to learn the secrets of TV football commentary. Commentators describe the action and provide information during matches to make the game more enjoyable for viewers watching at home. We'll see how they use colourful and creative language to maximum effect.

This is one lesson where you do need to talk in class. Speak up!

TRICKS OF THE TRADE

If you want to be a TV commentator, the following tips for your tongue should be on the tip of your tongue! At Football School, we call this the Guide for Orally Astonishing Language Skills, or GOALS.

1. LOVE YOUR LARYNX

Just as footballers ensure their bodies are in top condition before a game, commentators need to make sure their voices are well looked after. If it is cold, wear a scarf. Avoid smoky places, since this will protect your throat. Also, avoid shouting or whispering as you don't want to strain your vocal chords in the run up to the game.

2. DANNY, DRINK WATER!

Talking for 90 minutes at a time is tough on your throat, and you don't want it to dry out. No croaking please! To make sure your throat is well hydrated before the match, take small sips of water throughout the day and eat foods such as cucumbers, tomatoes, spinach and watermelon, which are full of water. Don't eat spicy foods, as they can irritate your throat. But don't drink too much – you don't have time to go to the loo mid-game!

3. PREP YOUR PENCIL CASE

This is one job where you need to bring a pencil case into work! Commentators have different coloured pens and highlighters to make notes on the team-sheets.

4. STUDY THE TEAMS

Draw a crib-sheet for both teams on a piece of paper. Put the players' names and numbers in their correct positions, and for each player add a relevant fact, just like we have done below. (We just did one team, but you will need to do both). Memorise the players' names and numbers. Look to see if any facts stick out.

DATE: Today

TEAM NAME: Commentary City

11
Diego Gonzalez
First Venezuelan in the League

9
Harry Dane
29 goals so far (2 hat-tricks, 5 headers)

10
Charlie Crosser
12 assists all with right foot

7
Lionel Tidy
Made Argentina debut last week

4
Edgar N. Forcer
First game after 6 month knee injury

8
Davie Disco
Scored 8 free kicks this season

3
Junior Tackles
Match debut, only 17

5
Bertie Boxer
Birthday today, aged 24

6
Cruncher Bones
5 red cards

2
Philip Fitness
Played every minute

1
Gary Gloves
Saved 3 penalties

5. PRACTISE PRONUNCIATION

Players come from all over the world and their names are not always easy to pronounce. It's always worth asking someone from a player's country of origin for the correct pronunciation, because different languages pronounce the same letters in different ways. Here is our list of five footballers who are most likely to get a commentator's tongue in a twist:

NAME	NATIONALITY	PRONUNCIATION
James Rodríguez	Colombian	Ha-mess Rod-ree-geth
César Azpilicueta	Spanish	Say-zar Ath-pili-coo-et-ah
Gonzalo Higuaín	Argentinian	Gone-zar-low Ee-gway-een
İlkay Gündoğan	German	Ilk-eye Gun-doe-wan
Toby Alderweireld	Belgian	Toe-bee Al-der-vay-reld

6. THINK ABOUT THE STORY

Consider the circumstances leading up to the game. What are fans interested in? Is it the World Cup final, a derby game between two local rivals, or is one of the coaches under pressure after a string of poor results? You need to have a firm grasp of the backstory to the match, since at the final whistle the fans don't just want to know the score, they want to know what the result means for them. United win the Cup! Rovers are relegated! The coach could now lose his job!

7. PUT THE KETTLE ON

The match is about to start. You have your pens, the team-sheet … all you need now is a cup of tea! Make yourself a herbal tea with honey and lemon, which will help soothe your throat once those vocal cords spring into action. Beware of drinking fizzy drinks while commentating, since they will put air in your stomach. You don't want to burp live on TV!

8. BE ENTHUSIASTIC (WITHIN REASON!)

To be a good commentator, not only do you need to be interested in football, you also need to *sound* interested in football. Your voice must be positive and enthusiastic. Do-not-speak-with-no-e-mo-tion-like-a-ro-bot. But don't go craaaaaazy! DON'T SHOUT! Don't start off too enthusiastic, because then how can you turn up the excitement when there is something really dramatic like a goal or a red card? We recommend starting at about 60 per cent volume, so you can scale it up to 100 per cent when a goal is scored. But don't get too excited – you need to remember to breathe!

Not everyone gets it right first time. Hundreds of viewers complained when former England player Phil Neville commentated his first game during the 2014 World Cup. They said he was boring! But he practised and improved.

In club football, fans of both teams may be watching so try not to favour one team over the other: regardless of the team you support, you must stay impartial. For international football, the rules are a bit different. If, say, England are playing another country, then the commentators for English TV will tend to favour England, because most of the viewers will be England supporters.

9. DON'T, UMM, HESITATE

Be confident with what you say and what you don't. Try not to use filler words, such as "umm", "err" or "like", in the middle of a sentence. These words mean nothing and get in the way of what you are trying to say. Here are a few techniques to avoid falling flat with fillers:

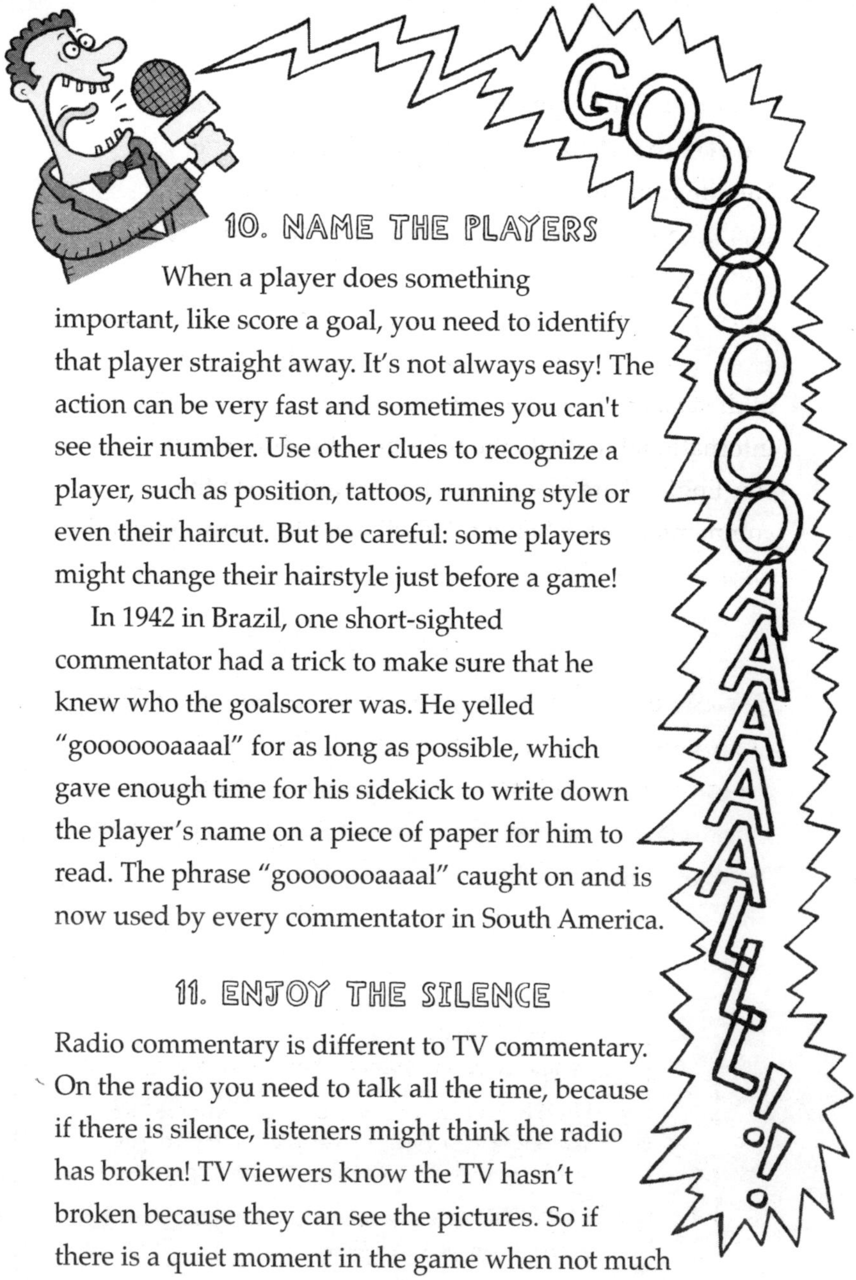

10. NAME THE PLAYERS

When a player does something important, like score a goal, you need to identify that player straight away. It's not always easy! The action can be very fast and sometimes you can't see their number. Use other clues to recognize a player, such as position, tattoos, running style or even their haircut. But be careful: some players might change their hairstyle just before a game!

In 1942 in Brazil, one short-sighted commentator had a trick to make sure that he knew who the goalscorer was. He yelled "gooooooaaaal" for as long as possible, which gave enough time for his sidekick to write down the player's name on a piece of paper for him to read. The phrase "gooooooaaaal" caught on and is now used by every commentator in South America.

11. ENJOY THE SILENCE

Radio commentary is different to TV commentary. On the radio you need to talk all the time, because if there is silence, listeners might think the radio has broken! TV viewers know the TV hasn't broken because they can see the pictures. So if there is a quiet moment in the game when not much action is happening, you don't need to describe it. You can keep silent for a few seconds, but stay on the ball!

12. ENHANCE THE PICTURES

The job of a TV commentator is to add to what you are already seeing. For example, if Luis Suárez passes the ball to Lionel Messi, you don't say, "Luis Suárez passes the ball to Lionel Messi," because everyone watching can see that! However, saying, "Messi makes an intelligent run into the space to receive Suárez's pass," gives additional information that helps the viewer understand the game in greater detail.

13. OH MY WORDS!

It's boring to listen to words that are repeated too often. A wide range of words will ensure that you always have a new one handy. The best way to develop your range, or **vocabulary**, is to read – and not just *Football School*! Any book or magazine will give you access to new words, and that's the best way for your brain to take them on board. One football writer calculated there are 73 different ways to describe how a goal is scored! These include:

Can you think of any more?

Now think of different ways you can describe a header that leads to a goal:

Crashing! Glancing! Towering! Angled! Diving!

As you can tell, we love words around here!

Commentators also use language creatively, for example by using **metaphor** and **simile**. A metaphor is a word or phrase that we use to describe something as if it was something else, so that it paints a picture of what's going on. For example, when we say that the Wembley pitch is a green carpet, we don't mean that the pitch is an actual carpet! We mean that it is neat, tidy and luxuriant like a brand-new carpet. When we say that the game is on a knife-edge, we do not mean that the game is literally on a knife-edge, we mean that it is dangerously balanced, as if on the thin edge of a knife.

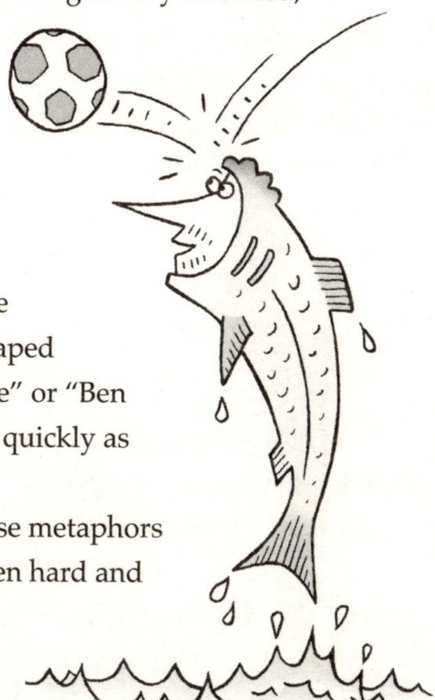

A simile is when we compare one thing with another, using the word "like" or "as", in order to make the description more vivid. For example, "Alex leaped like a salmon to head it home" or "Ben dribbled past his markers as quickly as an Olympic skier".

The best commentators use metaphors and similes all the time. Listen hard and see how many you can spot.

14. BE NATURAL

Commentators need to be able to think on the spot. If a good idea comes to you during the game, write it down. Ben's friend Dave commentated on Greece knocking out France at Euro 2004. Just before the end of the game, he thought of a joke based on the name of France's former general Napoleon Bonaparte. He used it on the final whistle: "Napoleon Blown Apart! France are out of the competition!" A joke that is a play on words is a pun. At Football School, we love puns!

If you get the giggles or need to cough while commentating, it's not the end of the world. We all do that too. One TV presenter told us: "When I have a laughing fit, I prefer to go with it and I just hope the viewers join in!" So go ahead ... LOL!

CLUELESS COMMENTATORS

Some commentators are remembered for saying silly things. Here are some examples of who said what, and why it was wrong:

TAUTOLOGY

When you say the same thing twice in different words.

CONTRADICTION

When you say two things that are the opposite of each other.

MALAPROPISM

When you use the wrong word in the place of a similar-sounding one.

ENGLISH QUIZ

1. What is tautology?

a) The study of tautology
b) When you say the same thing twice in different words
c) When you tie something up very tight

d) When you misremember a well-known phrase

2. Argentina captain Diego Maradona dribbled from inside his own half to score an outstanding goal in Argentina's 1986 World Cup quarter-final victory over England. Complete the line from English commentator Barry Davies describing the goal: "And you have to say that is..."

a) Annoying
b) Offside
c) Magnificent
d) Sick

3. What is the correct pronunciation of the first name of Belgium winger Eden Hazard?

a) Ee-den
b) Ee-dayn
c) Ay-den
d) Ay-dayn

4. Complete the following phrase that describes a goal scored confidently: "She finished that chance..."

a) With aplomb
b) With a plum
c) With a plop
d) With a pam-pam

5. How did American commentator Max Bretos describe a Paul Scholes goal scored for Manchester United against Liverpool in 2011?

a) He sang "Gol de Scholes" to the tune of "Eye of the Tiger".
b) He sang Paul Scholes to the tune of "Happy Birthday".
c) He sang "God Save Paul Scholes" to the tune of "God Save the Queen".
d) He sang Paul Scholes to the tune of "Despacito".

Monday
Lesson 5

PHYSICS

Professional footballers come in all sizes. Some players are short and others are tall. Just like your coaches at Football School! Alex is shorter than Ben, although he grows a little when his hair goes super curly.

This lesson is about height. On the pitch being tall is an advantage in some situations. In others, being short is better. We are going to learn about how our ability to run and dribble changes depending on our feet … and our height!

We will also meet the world-famous footballer who feared he was too small to make it, and the tallest and shortest nationalities in the world. That's the long and short of it. Now let's aim high!

THE BOY WHO WOULD NOT GROW

Lionel Messi is one of the world's greatest ever footballers. Many people think the Argentinean forward is the best player in the history of the game. But when he was younger, Messi had a medical condition and was worried that he might be too short to become a professional player. He also suffered at the hands of bullies who were mean about his height. His story can tell us a lot about the dedication and sacrifice he made at a young age to fulfil his dreams. And of course it shows us that great things can come in small packages!

Messi grew up in Rosário, a city in Argentina. He joined local team Newell's Old Boys when he was just six years old. His youth team won almost every game they played in. But by the time he was ten, all his teammates were growing taller much faster than he was.

When Messi failed to have a growth spurt, he visited Dr Diego Schwarzstein. The doctor diagnosed that Messi had a rare growth **hormone** disorder. Hormones are chemicals produced by our bodies that control how our body and emotions work. It turned out that Messi's **pituitary gland**, a pea-sized organ in the brain responsible for the balance of hormones, was not sending out the right amount of growth hormone. A lack of this hormone can lead to poor vision and lower immunity – issues that could have prevented Messi from turning professional. The doctor prescribed Messi with a three-year course of treatment.

It was a tough time. "Every night I had to stick a needle into my legs, night after night after night, every day of the week, and this over a period of three years," he said.

In the middle of his course of treatment, Argentina suffered from a financial crisis and Messi's family was no longer able to pay for the growth hormones. The treatment was expensive, costing around $1,000 per month. Newell's could not afford it, and nor could River Plate, another club who were interested in Messi. Only one team was prepared to sign Messi and take on the costs of the treatment for another year. That club was Barcelona. So aged just thirteen, he moved to a new country with his father Jorge.

Messi went on to make Barcelona the greatest team of his generation. He has won more than eight league titles, four Champions Leagues and three Club World Cup titles with Barcelona; and he has won the Ballon D'Or award for the world's best player five times. If you put all his trophies on top of each other, they would be taller than him!

Messi is now 1.70m (5ft 6ins) and taller than Diego Maradona, Argentina's former World Cup-winning captain. "I don't know if you will be better than Maradona, but you will be taller," Dr Schwarzstein had promised him. At Football School, we believe you should never give up on your dreams – and Messi has definitely reached the very top!

HOW MESSI HIT THE HEIGHTS

Messi, who is one of the best dribblers in the history of the game, is still shorter than the average footballer. His small stature is not unusual for these skills: many of the best dribblers in the game are also short.

Short people make better dribblers than tall people, because short people find it easier to control their balance when running with the ball than tall people. Tallies are more likely to topple, but shorties will usually stay up!

To understand why short people can control their balance better, we need to learn about the laws of **physics**. Physics is the study of how everything moves around the universe. And when we say everything, we mean EVERYTHING. Physicists are interested in the movement of big things like planets, small things like atoms … and medium-sized things like footballers.

A-MASS-ING

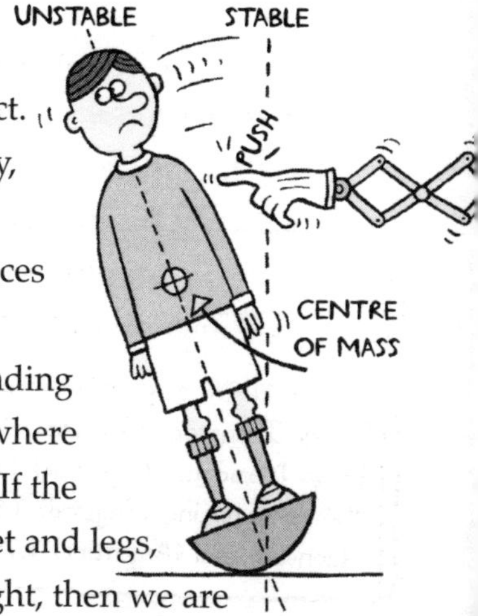

Mass is the amount of stuff in an object. The centre of mass, or centre of gravity, of an object is a point usually in the middle of that object. The object balances around this point.

The centre of mass of a human standing up is in the middle of the body, somewhere around the height of the belly button. If the centre of mass is directly above the feet and legs, as it is when we are standing up straight, then we are stable and we will not fall over.

But if the centre of mass is not directly above the legs and feet, such as when we are pushed, we are unstable and we will fall over, unless we move our centre of mass back between our legs and feet. We can return to stability by standing straight again, or by placing our legs further apart.

Now let's think about what a player is doing when they are dribbling with the ball. The player is constantly darting from side to side, speeding up and then slowing down. The centre of mass is moving all over the place, going from positions that are stable to positions that are unstable and back again.

SHORT AND STEADY

A short player has shorter, lighter limbs and so, in general, will find it easier to control their centre of mass than a tall player. For example, if a short player and a tall player lean forwards at the same angle, all other things being equal, the tall player will actually be leaning further than the short player, because the tall player has a longer body. This means the tall player is more likely to topple and has to use more energy to steady themselves. Small players spend less energy on maintaining stability, which means they can spend more energy on running, speeding up and controlling the ball.

If you look at how a tall player like Cristiano Ronaldo dribbles, you'll see he uses tiny steps. If he made big steps, he would be wasting lots of energy moving his large, heavy bones around to make sure he is stable. But a much shorter (and lighter) player, like Lionel Messi, dribbles using small steps or big steps – which is one of the reasons Messi is so hard to defend against. You never know which way he will go!

TALL ORDER

We've seen how shortness can be an advantage for dribblers. Now let's look at a position where tall is usually best: wearers of the number 1 shirt. As goalkeepers can use their hands, tall ones can usually reach higher to catch crosses that are intended for strikers.

But it is more than just feet and inches. Scientists have shown that taller people are better at judging distances, so they can more accurately identify the position of the ball. This may be because they are used to looking at the ground from further away.

HEIGHTOMETER

Scientists looked at the height of over 30,000 professional male players from 31 different European countries to calculate the average height of players by position:

Goalkeepers: 1.89m (6'2") Defenders: 1.83m (6'0") Midfielders: 1.79m (5'10") Forwards: 1.82m (5'10")

LOOKING HIGH AND LOW

Football has a huge variety of heights among its players. Other sports are better suited to tall athletes, while some to smaller athletes.

SPORT	AVERAGE HEIGHT
Basketball	2.00m (6'7")
Volleyball	2.00m (6'7")
American football	1.91m (6'3")
Ski jumping	1.75m (5'9")
Gymnastics	1.63m (5'4")

TAKING THE HIGH ROAD

Tottenham Hotspur's 9–1 Premier League win over Wigan in 2009 broke goalscoring records and made history for another height-related reason. Peter Crouch, one of the Premier League's tallest players at 2.01m (6′7″), opened the scoring. Aaron Lennon, who is 1.65m (5′4″), scored the fifth goal for Spurs: the teammates' height difference of 36 centimetres is the biggest in Premier League history!

HEADS YOU WIN!

Tim Cahill is one of the best headers in the history of football. The Australia midfielder is 1.78m (5′10″) tall, which makes him much shorter than most of the defenders he plays against. "I head a ball like someone else kicks it," he said. But how? First, he works hard in the gym, building power in his legs to give added spring to launch into the air, and upper body strength to keep defenders at bay. To get to the ball before taller defenders, he has to arrive in the right area at the perfect time. He puts out his arms as an elevation tool to propel him upwards and uses his neck muscles to direct the ball where he wants. He is also fearless when he jumps for the ball and he offers this advice to all future goal-getters: "Believe in your ability and place the ball out of the goalkeeper's reach."

ON A NATURAL HIGH

Here is where you will find the tallest, and the shortest, people in the world:

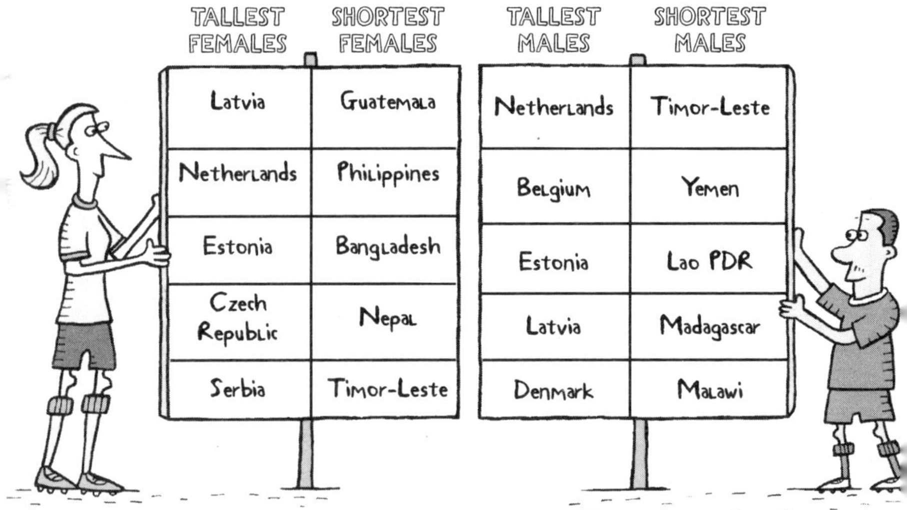

TALLEST FEMALES	SHORTEST FEMALES	TALLEST MALES	SHORTEST MALES
Latvia	Guatemala	Netherlands	Timor-Leste
Netherlands	Philippines	Belgium	Yemen
Estonia	Bangladesh	Estonia	Lao PDR
Czech Republic	Nepal	Latvia	Madagascar
Serbia	Timor-Leste	Denmark	Malawi

PHYSICS QUIZ

1. **What is the name for the point in an object about which it balances?**

a) Centre of mass
b) Centre of maths
c) Centre of gravy
d) Balance point

2. **Which diminutive Brazilian legend was known affectionately by his fans as "Shorty"?**

a) Pelé
b) Ronaldo
c) Romário
d) Ronaldinho

3. **The pituitary gland controls our growth hormones but where in the body is it?**

a) Under the arm
b) In the brain
c) Back of the throat
d) Heel of the foot

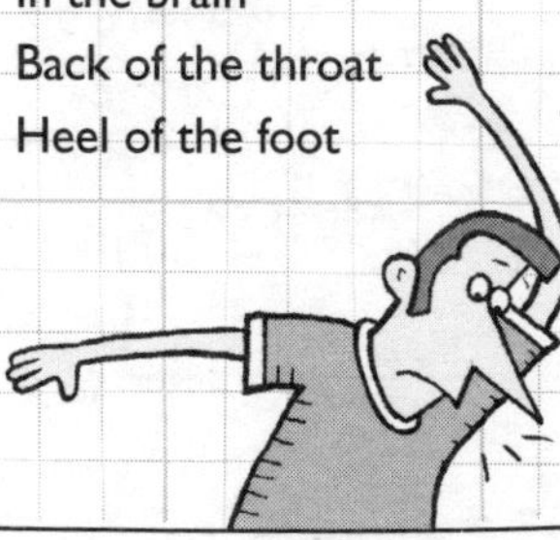

4. **A Dutch psychologist who studied the height of football referees discovered which one of these facts?**

a) There are more goals with shorter referees.
b) There are more penalties with taller referees.
c) Shorter referees control games better.
d) Taller referees control games better.

5. **Kristof Van Hout, a goalkeeper from Belgium, is thought to be the tallest professional footballer in the world. How tall is he?**

a) 2.08m (6'10")
b) 2.11m (6' 11")
c) 2.13m (7'0")
d) 2.16m (7'1")

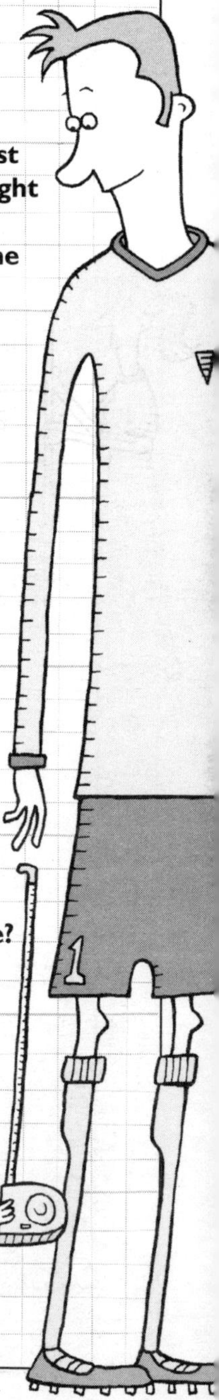

Tuesday
Lesson 1+2
ZOOLOGY
What's Benin?
A box?
No, it's a country!
In what country is Kampala the capital city?
Uganda?
You silly goose!

Go Lions! Go Elephants! Go Leopards!

No, we're not watching a wildlife documentary. We're cheering on some of our favourite African teams.

Football is the most popular sport in Africa, a continent made up of 54 countries and with a population of 1.2 billion people. Africans like Mo Salah of Egypt and Victor Moses of Nigeria are among the world's best players.

The national football teams of many African countries show their love for their continent's amazing wildlife by giving themselves animal nicknames. For example, Nigeria are known as the Super Eagles, Cameroon are the Indomitable Lions and Ivory Coast are the Elephants.

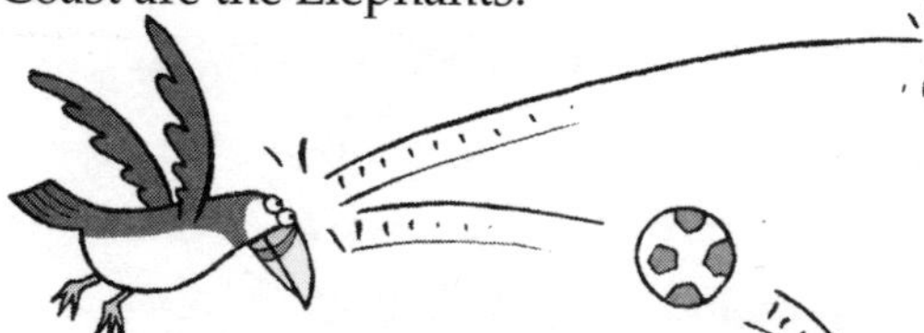

These animals are powerful symbols. Eagles fly high and swoop fast, lions prowl and devour their prey and elephants are the biggest land animal on the planet. Yet not every country has chosen a well-known animal for their team nickname. The continent is home to thousands of species of mammals, fish and bird, so there are some other amazing animals to choose from.

In this lesson, we're going to discover some of the more curious animals that are the nicknames for African national teams. Tweet! Bleat! Hiss!

ON THE WING

Country: Uganda

Nickname: The Cranes

Why? The grey crowned crane is the national bird of Uganda, appearing on its flag and coat of arms.

What are they? Cranes are tall birds, standing about a metre high, with long legs and long necks. In fact, the mechanical cranes you see on building sites are named after these birds because of their long necks. There are fifteen species of crane across the world, of which the grey crowned crane is one. Its wingspan is huge – up to 2 metres, as wide as the exceedingly tall footballer Peter Crouch is high. Grey crowned cranes live in grasslands and wetlands in eastern and southern Africa.

Distinguishing features? The grey crowned crane has one of the best haircuts in the animal kingdom: a frizzy gold crown that looks like a bleached-blond crimped perm, not unlike how many footballers used to look in the 1980s.

Animal behaviour: Cranes are famous for their elaborate dance routines, which they use to attract mates. These routines include bobbing their heads, fluttering their wings, twirling, jumping, bowing and running. When humans sing songs near them, cranes get into the groove by nodding their heads.

Clever birds: If a group of cranes are attacked by a predator, sometimes the adult crane will pretend it has an injury by limping in an exaggerated way so that the predator becomes interested in it, rather than the younger and more vulnerable chicks.

Would cranes be any good at football? Their long necks would make them good at heading. And their love of dance means they would have amazing goal celebrations. But they risk getting into trouble with refs for play-acting.

KEEP CALM AND CARRION

Birds are a popular nickname for many African nations. Apart from the crane, parrot and swallow, almost all are fierce birds of prey. These birds hunt and eat carrion (the word for rotting, dead animals). Feeling peckish, anyone?

Burundi: The Swallows
Mali: The Eagles
Sudan: The Jediane Falcons
Togo: The Sparrowhawks
Nigeria (men): The Super Eagles
Nigeria (women): The Super Falcons
Tunisia: The Eagles of Carthage
São Tomé and Príncipe: The Falcons and Parrots

HOOF IT UP

Country: Ethiopia

Nickname: The Walias

Why? The name comes from the walia ibex, which is a rare species of wild goat that only lives in Ethiopia.

What are they? The domestic goat we see on farms is actually only one of eight species of goat found around the world. Five of these goat species are mountain goats called ibexes. The walia ibex is the most endangered ibex species, with only about 500 animals left in the wild. Their population was much larger but they were killed by humans for their meat and fur. They are now only found in a small area of steep and jagged cliffs in Ethiopia's mountains, about 2,500 metres high, where it is hard for humans to capture them.

Distinguishing features: Male walia ibexes are about 1.4 metres tall and have light brown coats and white bellies. They also have enormous, curved horns, which can sometimes be more than 1 metre in length. Old males have thick black beards. The females are a lighter colour and a bit smaller, with thinner horns.

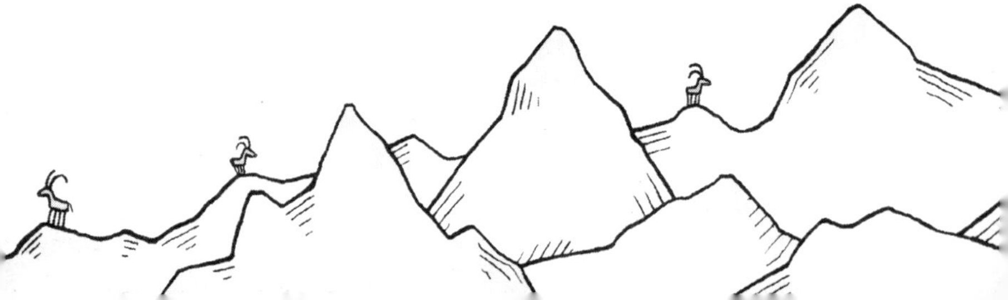

Animal behaviour: Ibexes are fantastic jumpers. They have to be, since they spend their days jumping up and down sheer cliff-faces looking for plants to eat. An ibex can jump about 2 metres high without a running start.

Smart footwear: An ibex hoof is the best climbing shoe in the animal kingdom. The hoof is made up of two thin toes, each with a sharp, jagged edge that is perfect for clinging on to tiny footholds on steep and rocky cliffs. A soft, textured underside presses against the rock to give extra grip.

Would walia ibexes be any good at football? They would be amazing at jumping for corners, although they would need to be careful not to puncture the ball with their horns. The sturdy grip of their hooves means they would never skid in the rain, but they may be more interested in climbing the stands than staying on the pitch.

PARKING ZEBUS

The ibex is a bovid, the name given to the family of hoofed, horned, grass-eating mammals that includes sheep, cattle, goats, buffalo, bison and antelopes. The munch bunch! Other African teams with bovid nicknames include:

Angola: The Sable Antelopes
Madagascar: The Barea (a species of zebu)
Niger: The Dama Gazelles

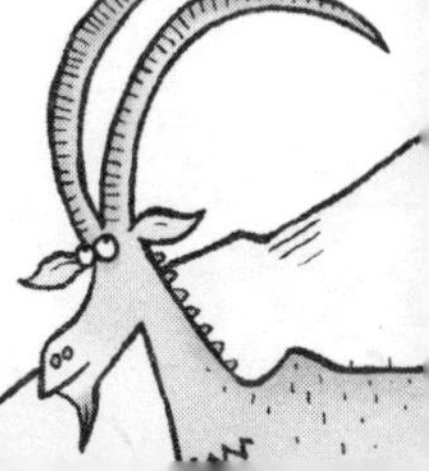

VENOM-ENAL

Country: Mozambique

Nickname: The Mambas

Why? Mambas are venomous snakes, meaning that they will bite attackers to inject **venom**, or poison, into them. Two of the four species of mamba live in Mozambique, including the black mamba, which is one of the most feared snakes in the world.

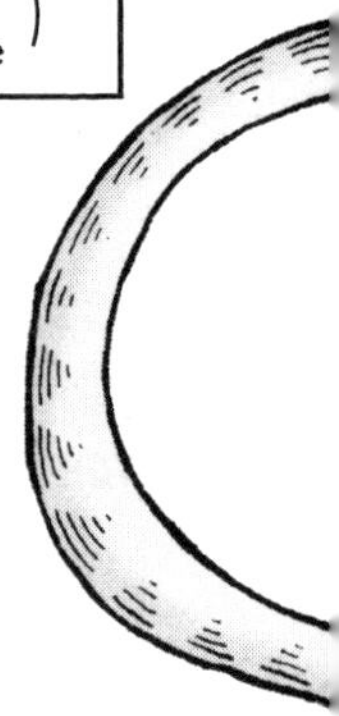

What are they? Black mambas are the longest snakes in Africa. Their average length is about 2 metres but they can grow to longer than 4 metres. Despite their name, they aren't actually black, but various shades of brown and grey.

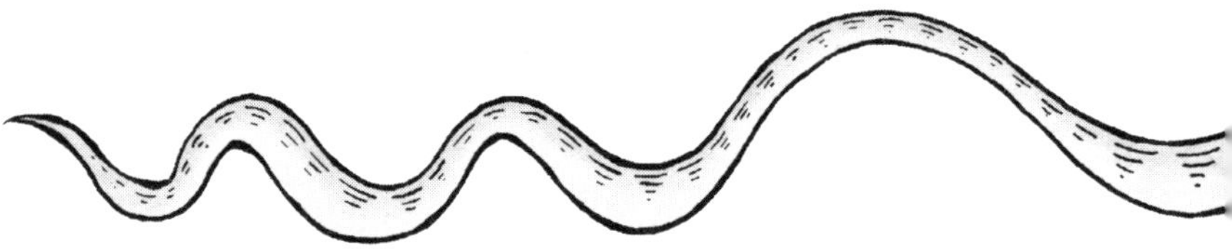

Distinguishing features? The insides of their mouths and tongues are completely black, as if they have been sucking an ink-flavoured lollipop. When threatened, they will open their mouths, revealing the black inside. This defensive posture is a warning that the mamba might bite. You don't want to be bitten by a black mamba! A few drops of their venom will kill you, sometimes in only half an hour.

Animal behaviour: The black mamba is the world's fastest snake. They can slither at around 12 miles per hour, which is about the same speed as a human running fast. While they zoom along, they hold their heads up a metre in the air, which adds to their menacing appearance.

Fearsome reputation: Mambas are feared throughout Africa and feature in many legends and myths. But even though they are deadly enough to kill a human, they are generally shy creatures who avoid threats.

Would mambas be any good at football? The snakes would be super speedy running up the wing and good at slithering past defenders. The opposition team would scarper in fear of being bitten. But not having any feet is a big barrier to footballing success.

INSECT-A-SIDE

Other animals as well as snakes have venom, such as spiders, bees and jellyfish. These two African national teams have chosen venomous nicknames. They certainly have sting!

Gambia: The Scorpions
Rwanda: The Wasps

GILL-INGHAM FC

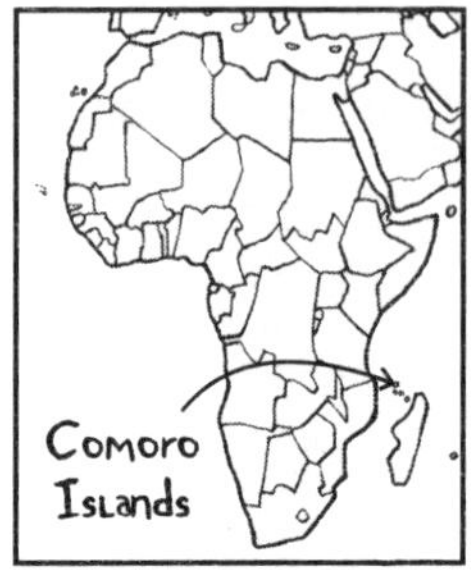

Country: Comoro Islands (or Comoros)

Nickname: The Coelacanths

Why? The coelacanth (which is pronounced *see-lah-kanth*) is a fish that lives in the ocean around the Comoro Islands, which are between Madagascar and the African mainland.

What are they? The coelacanth is one of the world's most fascinating fish. They are huge, growing up to 2 metres long. They weigh about 14 stone and are also famously ugly.

Distinguishing features? The coelacanth has been around since well before the dinosaurs, making it one of the world's oldest species of fish. They were first discovered as fossils. Scientists assumed that the fish had become extinct millions of years ago until one was discovered in 1938. Only about 500 of them are believed to still be in existence, making them one of the rarest fish in the world.

Animal behaviour: Coelacanths don't have fins like other fish. Instead they have four fin-like limbs that move one after the other, just like a trotting horse. The coelacanth helps us understand **evolution**, which is the process in which animals slowly change their characteristics over millions of years. For example, hundreds of millions of years ago there were fish in the sea but no animals living on the land. Gradually, some fish evolved and emerged from the water to become land animals. Some scientists believe that these first land animals evolved from fish like the coelacanth.

Fish-brained? The coelacanth brain is tiny, only taking up about 1.5 per cent of the space inside its skull. The skull also has a special hinge, so that when coelacanths open their mouths wide – to eat big fish – their skull splits in two.

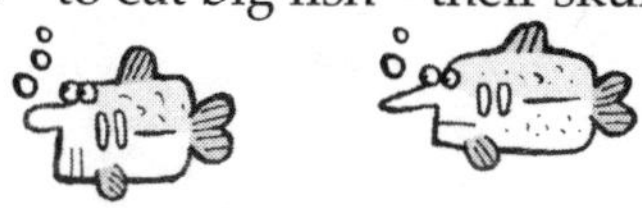

Would coelacanths be any good at football? Their limb-like fins make them the best underwater kickers of the ball, and their huge size and ugly appearance would scare opponents. But with their tiny brains and wide mouths, they might eat the ball (and the other players).

TEAMS WITH TEETH

The coelacanth has sharp enamel teeth to help it catch its dinner, but its gnashers are not the most feared in African waters. These two African teams have chosen underwater predators as their nicknames. They have bite!

Cape Verde: The Blue Sharks
Lesotho: The Crocodiles

MAMMAL MIA!

Mammals are a type of animal that are warm-blooded, have backbones and have either fur or hair, like cats, dogs … and humans. Most of Africa's best loved animals are mammals, like these ones:

BIG CATS

The lion is the largest of the big cats in Africa, and a symbol of strength and power around the world. It is therefore an obvious choice for a team nickname. Cameroon are the Indomitable Lions. Senegal are the Teranga Lions. (The word "teranga" means hospitality in Senegal's Wolof language, and reflects the country's pride in being welcoming and generous to visitors.) Morocco are the Atlas Lions, which is a subspecies of lion from the Atlas mountains, although none has lived in the wild there for almost a hundred years.

LITTLE FOXES

The fennec fox is a tiny animal, even smaller than the domestic cat, but that didn't stop Algeria, one of the most successful teams in Africa, choosing it as their nickname. The habitat of the fennec fox is the Sahara desert, which means it has to be tough to survive in extreme conditions. The fox's distinguishing feature is jumbo-sized ears, which help keep it cool by getting rid of excess heat.

TINY RODENTS

But the smallest of all the mammals used as a nickname was chosen by Benin and is … the squirrel! The first president of the Benin Football Federation suggested the name in the 1960s, since the squirrel is a plucky little thing that can climb high. However, many people in Benin feel that the team would perform better if they were named after a more aggressive, stronger animal, since bushy-tailed squirrels are unlikely to strike fear into the hearts of opponents. The sports minister has suggested the Emerging Panthers, and another suggestion was the Bees of Benin. Buzz buzz!

DEAD AS A DODO

An animal is considered **endangered** if there are so few of them left it is likely they will all die out. An **extinct** animal has died out. In the last 500 years, at least 250 species of animal have become extinct. The most famous of them, the dodo, lived on the island of Mauritius. This tubby bird with a long beak died out because humans destroyed its habitat and also killed it for food.

The Mauritius football team are nicknamed the Dodos, but this isn't because good footballers are an endangered species there, or possibly even extinct! The dodo is now a national symbol for the island, a reminder that animals can die out if we don't protect them.

ZOOLOGY QUIZ

1. Which of the following is a mammal?

a) A snake
b) A bee
c) A sea urchin
d) A whale

2. Cameroon are known as the Indomitable Lions. What does indomitable mean?

a) Impossible to defeat
b) Impossible to dominate
c) Impossible to eat
d) Impossible to catch

3. Which team has won the Africa Cup of Nations – the competition between the best African teams – the most times?

a) Egypt
b) Cameroon
c) Ghana
d) Nigeria

4. Guinea-Bissau are known as the Djurtus. What is a djurtu?

a) African wild guinea pig
b) African wild dog
c) African wild goldfish
d) African wild tortoise

5. The Liberian striker George Weah is the only African footballer to have won the FIFA World Player of the Year award, which he did in 1995. What new job did he take up in January 2018?

a) Coach of Liberian national team
b) Coach of Football School
c) Librarian
d) President of Liberia

Tuesday
Lesson 3+4
POLITICS
Why was the Spaniard lonely?
He was the only Juan there!
Are you for real?
No! I'm for Barça!
BARÇA

Which country is famous for bagpipes, berets and football? Not Scotland, not France, but Spain! The country is *mucho* brilliant at football, having won the World Cup in 2010 and the Euros three times, most recently in 2008 and 2012. Many top players, like David de Gea, Gerard Piqué and David Silva, are Spanish.

Spain is made up of many different regions, such as the Basque country (where they wear berets), Galicia (where they play the bagpipes) and Catalonia (where they dress up as cats – only joking!). In this lesson, we're going to discover how the politics of Spain – that is to say, how the country is organised into different regions – make its football so exciting. Whether in La Liga or on the European stage, the teams are unlike anywhere else in the world. *¡Bienvenido a España!*

THE REAL DEAL

Madrid is the capital of Spain, and the city's biggest football club is Real Madrid.

Originally, the team were called Madrid. But, in 1920, the King of Spain allowed the club to incorporate the Spanish word *real*, which means "royal", into their name. From their early days, the club were associated with the ruling class. They even started to use the crown in their team badge. What a crowning glory!

In the 1950s, Real Madrid won the first five editions of the European Cup, the competition we now call the Champions League. The club's number one fan, who was prepared to support Real Madrid over other Spanish teams, was the military leader of Spain at the time: General Francisco Franco.

Franco used Real Madrid's success, and the exhilarating way the team played, for his own political goals. His military government was deeply unpopular internationally because it was a **dictatorship**. This style of government is when a person or a small group rules with almost unlimited power and uses force to stop opposition. Franco used Real Madrid's wins to make Spain look like it was a thriving and exciting country with lots to offer, when actually it was a brutal and dangerous place to be if you opposed his rule.

With such powerful support, Real Madrid became one of the most famous things about Spain. No team has won the European Cup more times than they have and, in 2018, the team was the first to lift the Champions League trophy three seasons in a row. They are also one of the richest clubs in the world. That's real success!

Many people believe that the Spanish government still favour Real Madrid over the country's other teams. Opposition fans complained that during the Franco era, which lasted from 1939–75, referees always favoured Real Madrid. In one match against Barcelona in 1966, the referee played 11 minutes injury time and blew the final whistle as soon as Real Madrid scored the game's only goal. He claimed his watch had broken! Complaints about favourable treatment from referees continue today.

RIVAL ACTION

Real Madrid's biggest rivals are nearly 400 miles across the country: Barcelona.

In fact, the competition between the two clubs is probably the greatest footballing rivalry in the world, so much so that the match between them has its own name: *el clásico*, from the Spanish word meaning "classic", as in outstanding. The reason why Real Madrid and Barcelona dislike each other so much is a long story … so long it goes back centuries.

Barcelona is the second biggest city in Spain, and the capital of the region of Catalonia. About 800 years ago, the region became an independent country – the Principality of Catalonia – with its own laws, language and customs. But after a war in 1714, it became part of Spain. At the time, many Catalans did not want to be part of Spain – and over 300 years later, some still feel the same way.

The Barcelona football team has become a symbol of pride for the region. Barcelona have won over twenty Spanish league titles and, since 2000, four Champions League trophies. To many fans, every goal Barcelona scores against Real Madrid is a goal for Catalonia against Spain, as if the ancient war between them is still happening on the football pitch.

In recent years, many Catalans have wanted Catalonia to be independent again. The campaign for independence is the reason why if you watch a match at Barcelona's

Camp Nou stadium, you will notice that fans start chanting after 17 minutes and 14 seconds, which is to remember the year 1714.

Just as Catalonia has different customs to other parts of Spain, Barcelona makes a point of doing things differently to Real Madrid. While Real Madrid often (but not always) buy the biggest stars, known as *galácticos*, from around the world to win trophies, Barcelona focuses on teaching young players a possession-based style of play in their academy. The club encourages coaches to pick these local talents to represent the best of the region. Barcelona's most successful coach, Pep Guardiola, and two of its greatest players, Sergio Busquets and Xavi Hernández, are all born and bred in Catalonia.

Barcelona fans are proud of the differences between them and their great rivals from Madrid – especially when they are winning!

BEST OF FRENEMIES

Even though Real Madrid and Barcelona are fierce adversaries, when it comes to the Spain national team the clubs have to put their rivalry to one side. It can be difficult to play as a team alongside your arch-enemies, but the Spanish have shown it can be done! When Spain won the 2010 World Cup, NINE of the players who started the final played for either Real Madrid or Barcelona.

This spirit of friendship fell apart, though, after a series of particularly angry *clásico* matches in 2011, and defenders Sergio Ramos (Real Madrid) and Gerard Piqué (Barcelona) fell out. Luckily, the pair patched things up in time to help Spain win Euro 2012!

Spain has other hotly-contested local rivalries all over the country. These derbies are all big games:

MATCH	REGION
Real Oviedo v. Sporting Gijón	Asturias
Celta Vigo v. Deportivo La Coruña	Galicia
Athletic Bilbao v. Real Sociedad	Basque Country
Sevilla v. Real Betis	City of Seville
Las Palmas v. Tenerife	Canary Islands

WAKE ME UP BEFORE IAGO

Galicia is in the north-west of Spain, close to Portugal. Like other regions, it has its own language, its own customs and … its own weather: the coastal area is famous for being colder and wetter than the rest of Spain. Brrr!

Galicia also has its own fierce football rivalry, between clubs from the two most populous cities: Celta Vigo from Vigo, and Deportivo La Coruña from nearby A Coruña ("*A*" means "the" in Galician). Both used to compete in the Galician regional championship, but General Franco put an end to that competition in 1940.

Celta have never won a major trophy, while Deportivo were nicknamed Super Depor when they won their first and only La Liga title in 2000. With little chance of major trophies, these two teams put more emphasis on winning the local derby – victory counts as a good season for some fans!

One of those fans is Iago Aspas, who grew up in Vigo and started playing for Celta aged eight. He has scored some of the most important goals in the club's history and was top scorer in 2016, 2017 and 2018. He is loved because he has told the fans he will support Celta until the day he dies – and he would not even date a girl from A Coruña. True love!

BASQUING IN GLORY

The Basque Country is a region in the north of Spain, which is home to Athletic Bilbao, the club that sits third in Spain's all-time trophy table, after Real Madrid and Barcelona. (The Basque country also extends a little into the south-west border of France). Athletic is also the only team, apart from the big two, never to have been relegated from La Liga. Its record is particularly amazing because the club only picks players from the Basque Country, which has a collective population of about two million.

The other teams in La Liga choose players from anywhere in the world, which means they can choose from seven billion people. But gutsy Athletic have shown they are a match for the big fish by only playing local talent.

One of the reasons Athletic protects its Basque identity so fiercely is because of the way General Franco tried to stamp out Basque culture in the last century. Franco banned the use of the Basque flag and the use of the Basque language (Euskara) in public. But Franco's plan backfired. Now the Basque language is the region's main language, flags are everywhere and Athletic Bilbao is one of the strongest symbols of the Basque people. That's why you won't find Athletic ever signing a Brazilian wing-wizard or a tough-tackling Russian defender. It's the Basque way or no way!

How could Athletic Bilbao possibly be so successful with this approach? The club has actually found strength in being so selective:

1. Local pride
Athletic players grew up supporting the club and understand the fans because they are fans too.

2. Belief in a common purpose
Athletic players know that they don't just represent the club, or the city of Bilbao, but the whole idea of what it is to be Basque.

3. Winning is not the most important thing
Athletic fans want to watch local players in their team – even if they get relegated! Success comes from sticking to the Basque-only policy rather than the number of trophies that they win.

4. Continuity
Athletic mainly promotes players from its youth team, who already know the area, the tactics and their teammates. Not selling players can be more important than buying new ones!

WE WISH YOU A SMELLY CHRISTMAS

Catalans have a strange Christmas tradition: they have small figurines depicting a peasant doing a poo in their Nativity scenes. The tradition dates back to the eighteenth century, but no one is quite sure why it started. Some think the pooers, known as *caganers*, are fertilizing the earth, while others think it symbolizes equality: no matter how famous or successful you might be, you still need to poo. In recent years, Catalan shops have sold celebrity pooers, including members of royalty, American presidents and, of course, Barcelona players! Poo-ey!

POLITICS QUIZ

1. What does the Spanish word *real* mean in Real Madrid?

a) Rogue
b) Royal
c) Real
d) Rebel

2. What is the Guggenheim Bilbao, the city's most famous landmark?

a) A factory that makes footballs
b) A school where the uniform is the full Athletic Bilbao kit
c) A museum of modern art
d) A church where the organ player is the Athletic Bilbao goalkeeper

3. What is celebrated on 11 September every year in Barcelona?

a) Johan Cruyff's birthday
b) Ham Day
c) National Day of Catalonia
d) National Football Day

4. What is the Basque sport of bale-lifting?

a) Lifting a bale of hay as many times as possible in a set time
b) Stealing as many hay bales as you can from a farm before the farmer spots you
c) Squeezing as many hay bales as possible in a lift

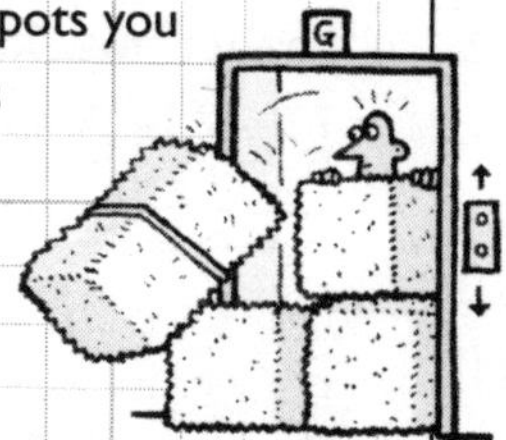

d) Lifting Gareth Bale as many times as possible in a set time

5. What happens at the annual La Tomatina festival in the Spanish town of Buñol?

a) Over 20,000 people throw tomatoes at each other in the town square
b) All greengrocers give out free tomatoes for a day
c) Everyone in Buñol must wear something red for the day
d) People called Tom or Tina come from all over the world to take part in a huge outdoor disco

Tuesday
Lesson 5

PSHE

Wakey, wakey! Let's start this lesson with a question: what does everyone need to perform at their best, whether it's Harry Kane getting ready to play in a World Cup game, Alex playing dominoes with Pelé or Ben running with his dog in the park? No dozing at the back! The answer is: sleep.

Everyone needs a good night's sleep and in this lesson we are going to learn how to get the most out of our *zzzzzs*. Professional footballers have to play matches at all hours: at lunchtime, in the afternoon and even late at night. They need to be getting enough sleep to be alert no matter what time it is.

We're going to find out what tricks they use to get the best night's sleep before a big game. We'll also meet the man who tells Real Madrid's players what pyjamas to wear. And the animal that sleeps for only two hours every day.

Rise and shine!

SLEEPY HEADS

When we go to sleep, we feel our mind slowly drifting off … and off … and off... Meanwhile, our body is getting to work. Because when you sleep, lots is happening.

- The heart slows, blood pressure lowers, the body's temperature drops and the blood supply to the muscles increases. This helps restore our energy levels when we wake.
- Chemicals are released to repair injured cells in the body. This helps the body protect itself against illness and recover from injury.
- The brain lists all the things that have happened that day in the part that stores memories.

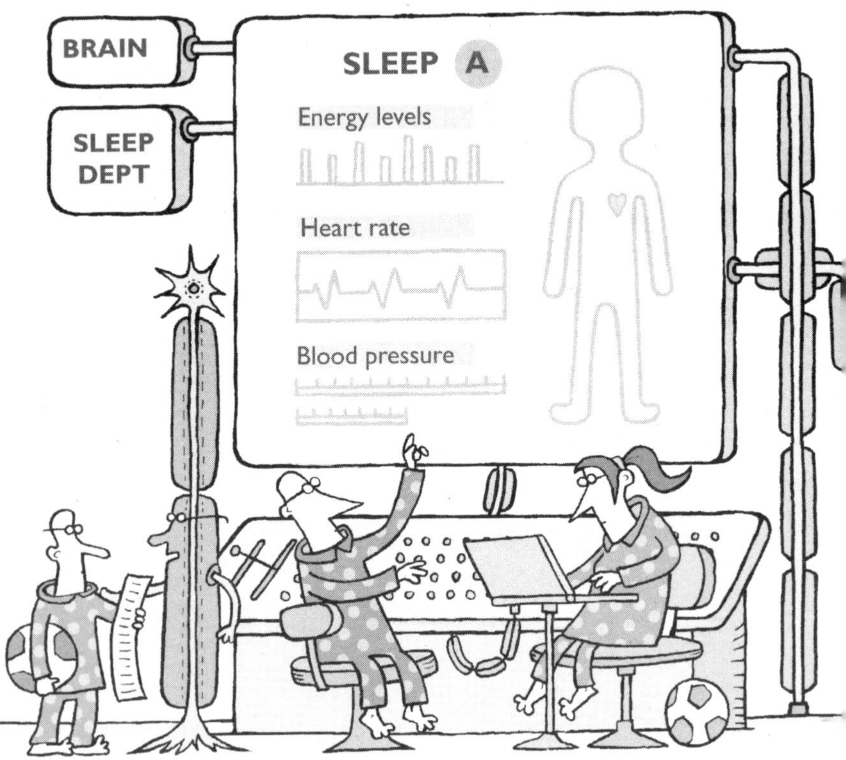

Sleep is our daily recovery and rejuvenation routine. Recently, scientists have discovered just how important sleep is, not only to our health but also to our happiness. They say that the right amount of sleep can help us live longer, be happier, more driven and creative and even more honest. Tell that to your parents when they try to wake you up!

Sleep can make a massive difference to sportspeople too. Footballers who sleep soundly have better reaction times and decision-making skills, and also recover more quickly from injury than those who toss and turn. Before we meet the man who teaches footballers how to sleep, let's learn about what happens when we are counting sheep... Baa-ck to bed!

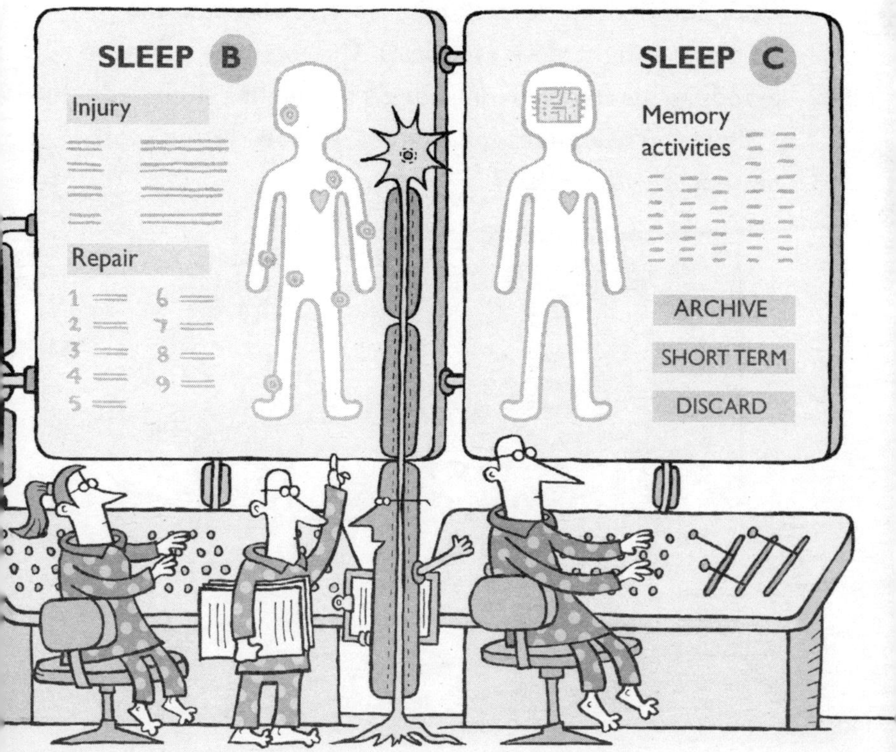

FIVE-A-NIGHT

When you're asleep, your body goes through a cycle of four different stages. Each stage serves a specific purpose, and each complete cycle lasts around 90 minutes – the same time as a football match!

You go through many **sleep cycles** in a night. Doctors say that four year olds need about twelve hours sleep a night, eight to twelve year olds need about ten hours and adults need about eight hours.

But it is not just about the number of hours, it is also about the quality of the sleep. **Deep sleep** is the most restorative sleep for your body, and the longer that period is, the better you will feel the next day. Babies spend a lot of time in deep sleep. But the older you become, the longer your **light sleep** cycle lasts. This might be why your grandparents complain of having a bad night's sleep.

So if you're a professional footballer, how do you get the most out of your *zzzzzs*?

SLEEP DIARY

Stage 1: TRANSITIONAL PHASE

About 5 minutes

The mind drops off. The eyes might roll. The muscles might jerk as you enter a light sleep.

FUNCTION: To prepare the body for sleep.

Stage 2: LIGHT SLEEP

About 45 minutes

The muscles relax, the mind rests and the heart-rate slows down. You can be easily woken from this stage.

FUNCTION: To repair damaged cells.

Stage 3: DEEP SLEEP

About 20 minutes

This is the most refreshing part of sleep. Breathing slows. The body is still. Sometimes your limbs will move, so this is when sleepwalking, talking in your sleep or bed-wetting can occur.

FUNCTION: This is the key stage for your body and mind to recover. The brain gets a reboot so it can learn afresh the next day. If you are a child, this is when your body grows.

Stage 4: REM (Rapid Eye Movement) SLEEP

About 20 minutes

The brain is active and revitalized. The body is still apart from your eyelids, which flutter. The heart-rate and blood pressure increase. You dream. The length of this stage increases with each cycle, so longer dreams occur towards the end of sleep.

FUNCTION: To store memories, as the brain processes our emotional experiences.

ASLEEP ON THE JOB

Nick Littlehales was working for a mattress company when he wrote to former Manchester United coach Sir Alex Ferguson, offering to help players recover from matches with sleep advice. Ferguson was keen to know more. Littlehales suggested that defender Gary Pallister, who was suffering from back problems, change his mattress. His advice also helped Ryan Giggs play for United even after he had turned 40.

That's how Littlehales started his new job as a sleep coach for the world's biggest football teams, including Chelsea, Real Madrid and the England national team.

Our body regulates its own feelings of sleepfulness and wakefulness according to natural light. When it is dark outside, we are more likely to want to sleep. When it's light, we want to be active. Littlehales visits each player's bedroom to make sure they have a good set of curtains and don't have too many distractions. One player he visited had four different flatscreen TVs on his bedroom wall, while another had a huge lit-up aquarium. Lights out!

TEACHING RONALDO TO SLEEP

When Littlehales was at Real Madrid, he knew that Cristiano Ronaldo was looking to improve all aspects of his performance, including his recovery and sleep. He gave tips to the players and coaches at Real Madrid and is proud that Ronaldo has adopted the principles of his advice. This is what he told European football's most successful club:

- Switch off all devices – such as laptops, smartphones and tablets – over an hour before you go to sleep. The blue light from these devices triggers brain waves, which makes it harder to go to sleep.
- Move from a warm, light area to a cooler, darker one. This recreates the everyday process of sunrise and sunset, as your brain slowly relaxes from hyper-awake mode.
- Avoid fatty or sugary foods in the evening as they take longer to digest. A balanced diet, which includes carbohydrates such as pasta, and protein such as chicken and nuts, will improve sleep quality.
- Sleep in the foetal position, which is curled up like a baby in their mother's stomach. This protects your vital organs. Lie on your non-dominant side. If you are right-handed, then lie on your left side: this position leaves your strong side free.

MORNING LARKS AND NIGHT OWLS

We're all different – and this is also true when it comes to sleep. Alex likes to get up at a time so early that most of us are still asleep. He's a morning lark. Ben prefers to go to bed later and wake up later in the morning. He's a night owl. What are you?

Your preference for certain sleeping patterns is based on an internal clock inside your body. This is known as your body clock, or **circadian rhythm**. Studies have shown that sportspeople reach their peak performance depending on their circadian rhythms. This information can be important for coaches as it will help them get the best out of their team.

SLEEPING PATTERN	BEST PERFORMANCE
Morning Lark	6-7 hours after waking up
Night Owl	11 hours after waking up

SIESTA FIESTA

We didn't always save sleep for one long session at the end of the day. Historians believe humans used to sleep for a bit, then get up in the middle of the night to do jobs, before going back to sleep again. Some experts believe that this is still the best way for the body to regularly recover. In certain cultures, particularly in hot countries like Spain or Greece, a midday nap is normal. This is known as a **siesta**. Swansea City have even encouraged their players to have daytime naps by installing sleep pods at the training-ground.

CLEAN ROOM, CLEAN MIND

Some people count sheep, others read until they drop their books. But England's record goalscorer Wayne Rooney used to put on the vacuum cleaner before he went to sleep! The repetitive and monotonous sound it made, known as **white noise**, drowned out other sounds that might keep him awake. When that didn't work, he would use his girlfriend's hairdryer – sometimes until it broke!

SLEEPOVER

The majority of athletes find it difficult to fall asleep before a big event. One club, Southampton, used to take custom-made mattresses to hotels for away games, so players would be used to the beds despite the unfamiliar environment. Another club, Bournemouth, give their players a sleep pack containing amber-lensed glasses, an eye mask and a small torch. The glasses, to be worn two hours before going to sleep, block out the harmful blue light from TVs and devices. The eye mask keeps out the light once the players are asleep and does not touch the eyelids, which can wake them up. The torch gives enough light so players, if they wake in the middle of the night, can go to the loo without turning on the main lights.

COUNTING SHEEP

Animals also need different amounts of sleep. Look at how long certain species sleep for in a 24-hour cycle:

ANIMAL	AVERAGE LENGTH OF SLEEP (PER 24 HRS)
Giraffe	2 hours
Horse	3 hours
Elephant	4 hours
Python	18 hours
Aldabra tortoise	18 hours
Brown bat	20 hours

PSHE QUIZ

1. The dream stage of sleep is called REM. What does REM stand for?

a) Really Extraordinary Memories
b) Rest, Exhale, Motionless
c) Rapid Eye Movement
d) Ready for Exciting Missions

2. How does Manchester City keep their recovery rooms dark, so players can rest properly?

a) All the lightbulbs are removed
b) There are blackout curtains over the windows
c) The rooms are underground
d) They make the players wear blindfolds

3. What was French midfielder Julien Faubert accused of doing when playing a match for Real Madrid against Villarreal in 2009?

a) Missing the game as he fell asleep in his car on the way to the stadium
b) Falling asleep in the dressing-room at half-time
c) Falling asleep on the substitutes' bench
d) Falling asleep on the pitch as soon as the final whistle blew

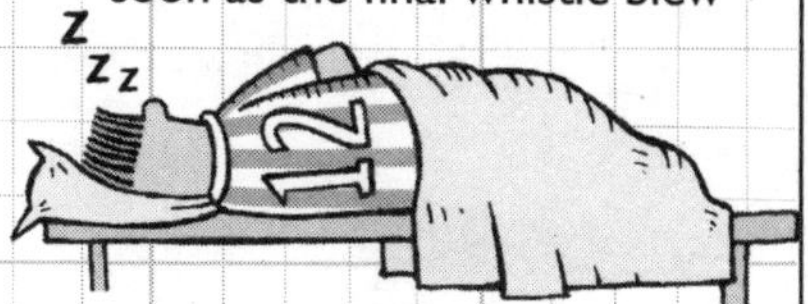

4. How long did Ghana midfielder Michael Essien, a Premier League title winner with Chelsea, say he needed to sleep for every night?

a) 4 hours
b) 8 hours
c) 10 hours
d) 14 hours

5. What causes snoring?

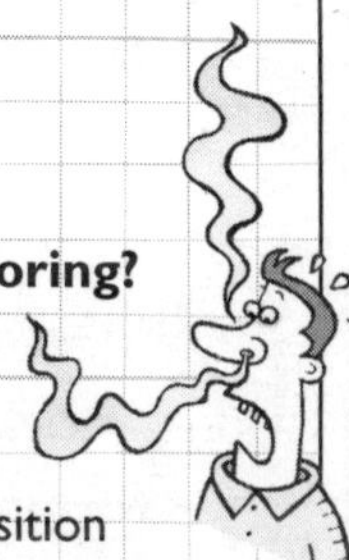

a) Your nose farting
b) Lying in an uncomfortable position
c) Your throat or nasal airways vibrating as you breathe
d) Reading *Football School* before bed

FOOTBALL SCHOOL

VISIT TO FOREST GREEN ROVERS FOOTBALL CLUB

Dear Parent/Guardian,

Your child is going on a school trip. The topics that will be covered:

Burping cows

Farting bugs

Flushing toilets

Mode of transport: electric bus
Please bring: notepad made from recycled paper, biodegradable rubbish bag
Don't bring: plastic packaging, pets, footballs
A lunch of fungus will be provided. Water will be available all day, served in recycled plastic bottles.

Kind regards,
Alex and Ben

I give permission for .... to take part in the school trip and promise that they will limit the singing of football songs to the bus trip, refrain from playing football using cowpats and will make a list of green goals at the end of the day.

Parent/Guardian signature:.......................................

We're travelling today to Nailsworth, a small town in the Gloucestershire countryside. It's the home of Forest Green Rovers, a club which in 2017 was promoted to the English Football League for the first time in their history.

Forest Green is very different from any other club – not just in England but anywhere in the world. They like to do things their own way. In fact if you look out of the bus window, you'll see they are so concerned about being different, that the name of the road that leads to their stadium is called Another Way!

Forest Green want to do things differently by looking after the planet as much as possible.

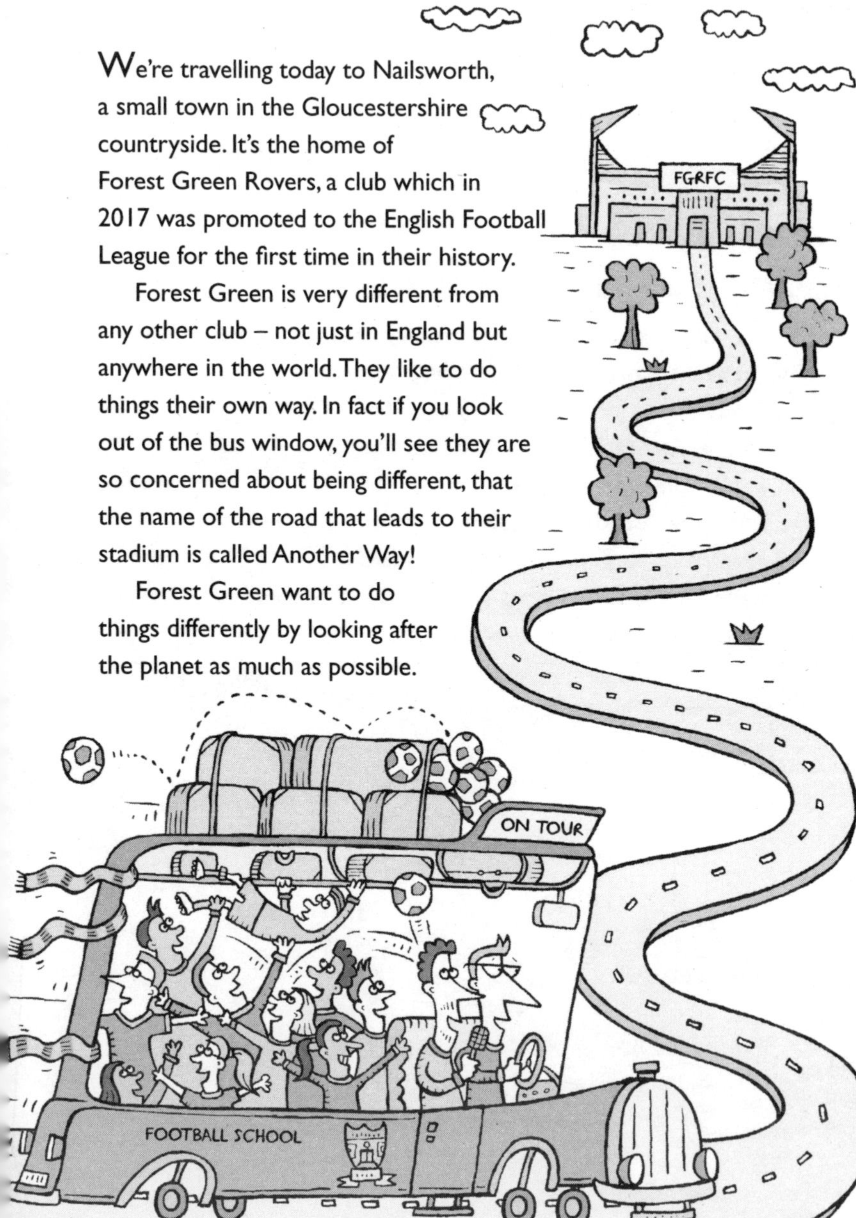

FOOTBALL TO THE RESCUE

Forest Green wants to save the world! But before we get off the bus and begin our visit to the club, let's look at two reasons why the world needs saving in the first place.

PROBLEM 1: CLIMATE CHANGE

The world is heating up, which is causing many problems. The ice at the North and South Poles is melting, which means that polar bears may soon lose their homes. We can't bear it! And, because the water from the melting ice is going into the world's oceans, the height of the sea, or **sea level**, is rising. If the sea level continues to rise, many villages, towns and cities all over the world could flood and eventually go underwater. Glug!

The major cause of **climate change** is the burning of fuels such as petrol and coal. (These substances are known as **fossil fuels**, because they are made over millions of years from dead plants and animals being crushed and heated underground.) When fossil fuels are burned, they create a gas – carbon dioxide – that ends up trapping heat in the Earth's atmosphere, making the planet hotter.

PROBLEM 2: PLASTIC POLLUTION

Plastic is fantastic! It is long-lasting, cheap and useful for so many things. But these reasons also make plastic really bad for the environment. For example, huge amounts are thrown away every day, and since it is long-lasting and does not rot, it ends up in rivers, on beaches and in the oceans, where it is a danger to sharks, fish, whales and other marine animals. The plastic problem is drastic!

CHANGE THE WORLD

We could reduce the problem of climate change if we stopped burning petrol and coal. And we could greatly reduce the problem of plastic pollution if we stopped using things made from plastic.

Sounds easy! But it is impractical and unrealistic to think we can instantly give up petrol, coal and plastics. We'd also have to give up travelling by plane, ship and most cars, since they use petrol. And we use plastics every day in hundreds of ways, from your toothbrush to your water bottle. Our way of life relies on substances that are damaging the world.

But we need to look after our planet better than we have been doing. We are going to have to change our behaviour by reducing our dependence on fossil fuels and throwing away less stuff that may be harmful to animals.

Forest Green Rovers are leading the way in doing both these things – and more. Let's start our first worksheet and find out how.

WORKSHEET 1: ENERGY

The electricity that we use when we switch on the lights comes from many different energy sources. In the UK, about half of our electricity comes from burning fossil fuels in power stations. Fossil fuels are **non-renewable**, which means that they will run out and take millions of years to be replaced. But electricity can also be made from **renewable** sources, which will not run out and can be used again and again. One shining example is the sun!

A **solar panel** is a shiny panel that absorbs sunlight and turns it into electricity. The New Lawn, the Forest Green stadium, has 170 solar panels on its roof, which provide the club with free electricity.

The advantages of solar power are that sunlight is free and the panels create no fumes or waste gases when they are used. The disadvantage is that it needs to be sunny! Sunny countries have lots of solar panels. The largest single "farm" of solar panels is in India and covers an area about the size of 6,500 football pitches.

Other renewable sources of energy are:

☐ Wind ☐ Waves ☐ Heat from underground rocks

WORKSHEET 2: PESTICIDES

In order to grow as much food as possible, farmers often use chemicals on their crops. **Fertilizers** help the crops grow and **pesticides** kill weeds and bugs that might eat the crops. The same is true of a football pitch. To get perfect luscious green grass, most grounds teams will also use fertilizers and pesticides.

But many fertilizers and pesticides contain chemicals that are harmful to humans and animals. Pesticides can kill insects such as bees, which are important to the environment. And, when the chemicals enter the soil, they don't just stay there. They get washed into rivers and may ultimately end up in the ocean, where they can harm fish. Traces can even be found in drinking water.

At Forest Green, the grounds team don't use pesticides and they only use fertilizers that are not harmful to humans and animals. These three options are all on the menu:

☐ Tea for bugs who then fart out gas that strengthens the roots

☐ Vinegar to kill off weeds

☐ Sugar and seaweed to feed the grass

WORKSHEET 3: SAVING WATER

A guiding principle of Forest Green is that you should never waste resources. Waste not, want not! That's why they collect their own rainwater. Some is saved from the stadium roof and some from sloping drains below the pitch, which flow into groundsman Adam Witchell's water tank. When full, the water tank can hold up to 73,500 litres, which is enough water to fill over 600 bathtubs.

Adam aims to collect enough rainwater for free so that he can water the pitch using the club's own reserves without ever switching on the water tap. Last season he almost managed it. The only time he turned on the tap was during a summer heatwave.

At Football School, we agree with Forest Green's message of never wasting water. Most of us use a huge amount of water every day without realizing it. One way to cut down on water is to always take a shower, not a bath. Look how much water you save:

☐ Bath: 115 Litres

☐ Shower: 50 Litres

☐ Toilet flush: 6 Litres

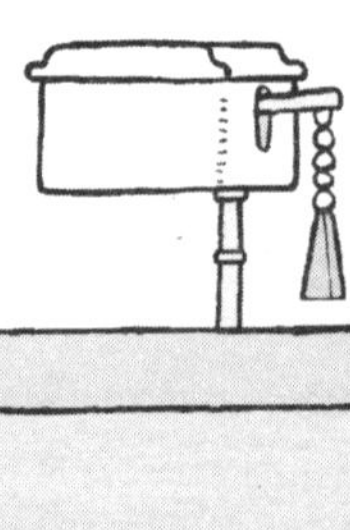

WORKSHEET 4: EATING GREEN

Fancy a meat pie at half-time? Sorry, you're out of luck! At Forest Green, meat and fish are banned. Instead, hungry fans are offered a Q-Pie, which is made from Quorn, a well-known meat substitute that is made from a fungus.

Meat is banned because of the effect that the meat industry is having on the planet. Farming animals uses a lot more land, feed, and water than farming the same amount of vegetables and grains. The high cost to the planet of eating meat has made some people decide to eat no meat products at all. People who don't eat meat are **vegetarians**, and people who don't eat meat or any other animal by-products, such as eggs and milk, are called **vegans**. Here are three international foods that vegans love:

☐ **Tofu:**

Semi-solid soya bean milk, from East Asia

☐ **Quinoa:**

Tiny plant seeds used as an alternative to rice, from South America

☐ **Freekeh:**

A nutty grain also used as an alternative to rice, from the Middle East

Cows are especially bad for the environment because of their burps! Cows belch a gas called **methane**, which, like carbon dioxide, makes the world get hotter. There are about 1.4 billion cows in the world, and the combined mega-burp of 1.4 billion cows is big, as well as stinky!

WORKSHEET 5: POLLUTION

Most cars use petrol, which, as well as pumping out carbon dioxide, also release dangerous chemicals into the air that can cause breathing problems in humans. This is known as **air pollution**.

In the last few years, car companies have been designing cars that run on electricity, which creates no exhaust fumes at all. Some drivers already using electric cars are … the players of Forest Green Rovers, after a company gave each of them an electric car for six months.

Electric cars are still more expensive than petrol cars, so less people drive them, but it is likely that this will change in the next ten years or so. In the near future, it's predicted that most cars will be fume-free.

Forest Green Rovers aren't just petrol-free on the road, but on the pitch too. They use a self-driving lawnmower that uses GPS to work out where it's going. It doesn't run on petrol, like many stadium lawnmowers do, but instead on solar-powered electricity. If it bumps into an object, it will back up and mow somewhere else. It takes three days to mow the whole pitch and it will text the grounds team if it gets into trouble. We hope it uses an e-mow-ji!

FOOTBALL SCHOOL GREEN GOALS

To finish off our trip to Forest Green, we spoke to Dale Vince, the owner of Forest Green Rovers. "We care deeply about the environment and want to show that football can also care for the world around us," he said.

The club is helping to protect the planet by: recycling as much as they can, not putting harmful chemicals into the ground, limiting the amount of carbon dioxide pumped into the air, and using renewable sources such as sunlight and rainwater. Often people use the word green to describe these types of environmentally friendly activity. FIFA has called Forest Green the greenest club in the world!

Dale told us that the club can become even greener, which is why he wants to build a new stadium made almost entirely out of wood. Wood is a renewable material, since trees can be replanted, unlike concrete and steel. Go Dale, we be-leaf in you!

This trip has taught us that we can all become greener. Here's a checklist of green goals that can help the planet. What else can you add to the list?

- **Re-use plastic bottles**
- **Recycle all paper**
- **Walk or cycle instead of using a car**
- **Turn the TV off after *Match of the Day***

WHAT A LOAD OF RUBBISH

Cristiano Ronaldo scored both goals when Real Madrid beat Sporting Gijón in the Spanish league in November 2016 – but some people thought he looked like total rubbish! The reason? Real Madrid were wearing shirts made from plastic rubbish that had been found on the coast around the Maldives Islands in the Indian Ocean. They had the message "For the oceans" on the neck of the shirt. The team were highlighting an important cause: when you throw plastic away it can end up in the ocean, where it can kill marine animals. It can cause problems for humans too: if we eat fish that has swallowed plastic, we could become ill as a result. A solution: make sure you recycle your plastic bags and bottles, don't throw them in the bin!

SCHOOL TRIP QUIZ

1. What piece of equipment turns sunlight into electricity?

a) Sunglasses
b) Sun hat
c) Sun cream
d) Solar panels

2. One of the biggest surges in demand for electricity in UK history occurred immediately after England lost a penalty shoot-out to West Germany in the 1990 World Cup semi-final. Why?

a) About a million people put the kettle on to make a cup of tea.
b) About a million people put the toaster on to have marmalade on toast.
c) About a million people phoned each other to commiserate.
d) About a million people turned up the TV volume to maximum when the BBC played the national anthem.

3. If we keep on using plastic at the same rate as we do now, which one of these will come true?

a) By 2020, all football stadiums will be made of plastic.
b) By 2030, we will drive in plastic cars.
c) By 2040, we will be born with plastic heads.
d) By 2050, there will be more plastic in the ocean than fish.

4. Which striker claimed he started scoring more goals after he turned vegetarian?

a) Harry Kane
b) Romelu Lukaku
c) Sergio Aguero
d) Neymar

5. Which of the following is a recommended way to save energy?

a) Turn out the lights when you leave a room
b) Eat more bananas
c) Wear underpants on your head
d) Sleep all day

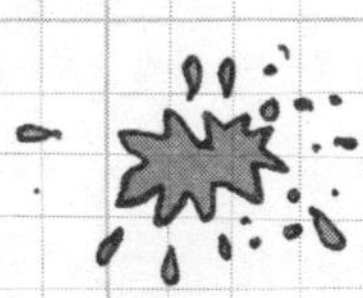

Thursday
Lesson 1+2

HISTORY

This lesson we're going back in time: way back to Sheffield in the 1850s, when two smart people had an idea that changed the world. Can you guess what it is? It has brought joy and sometimes sadness to millions of people all over the world. Nope, it's not Football School. But without these two pals, Football School might not exist.

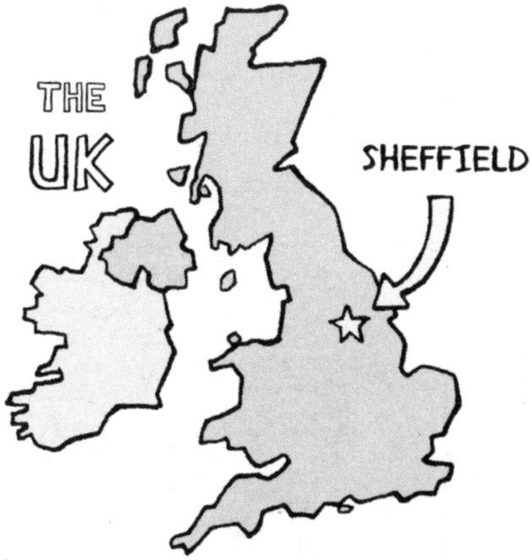

Let's step into the time machine!

WHERE IT BALL BEGAN

One sunny day in the summer of 1857, two friends went for a walk in the countryside just outside the city of Sheffield in the north of England. William Prest, a wine merchant aged 25, and Nathaniel Creswick, a lawyer aged 26, were both athletic and loved sports.

On this particular walk, they chatted about two of the most popular sports of that time: fencing and cricket. They also talked about a new sport, football, which was being played at schools such as Eton and universities such as Cambridge. Each school had their own version of the rules of football, and before every match, the captains would agree on the rules for that particular game. But imagine playing a game when every time you play, the rules would change slightly – confusing!

The friends decided that football would be a good sport for the people of Sheffield if only there were some organized rules that every team could follow. So they wrote to all the schools to find out their rules. "What a lot of different rules we received," said Creswick. There wasn't even a defined length of time for matches. "We generally played until it was dark," wrote one school.

The friends took the best suggestions and started to write down a version of the rules they were both happy with. A few months later, on 24 October 1857, they founded Sheffield Football Club, the first football club in the world. The club's purpose was to get people together to play football over the winter months when no one was playing cricket.

In 1859, Prest and Creswick finalized their rulebook, which they handed out to all members of their new club. Here are some of the rules:

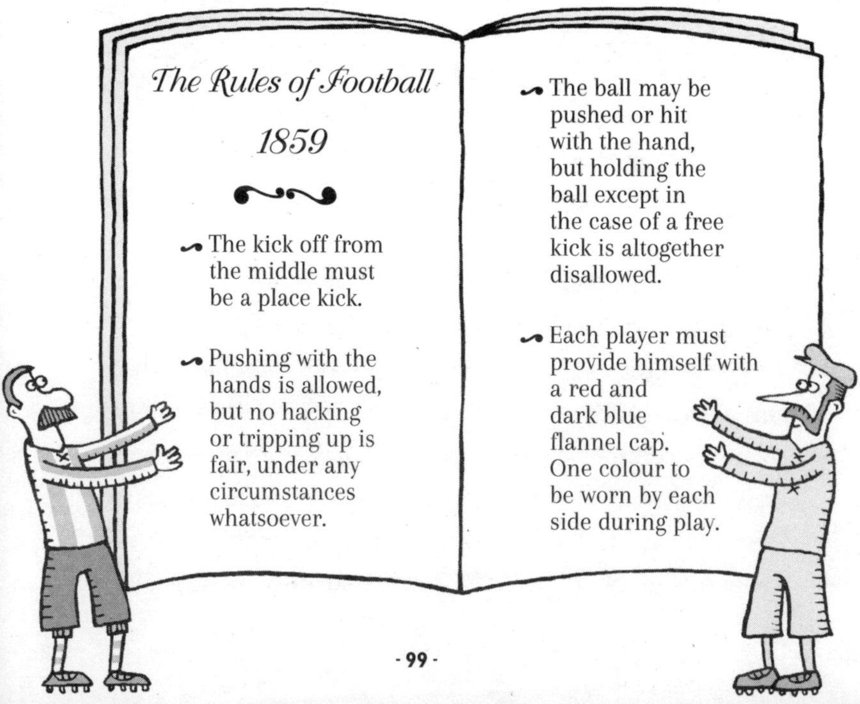

GOLDEN RULES

The Sheffield FC rulebook from 1859 is the foundation of the game as we know it today. Only once there were written-down rules that everyone agreed on, could football grow from schools and universities to become a national – and then a global – sport.

Some of the rules have changed since 1859, such as the ones about pushing the ball with the hands or wearing flannel caps, but, even so, the Sheffield FC rulebook was a landmark moment in footballing history. It set the future course for the game, most notably because, even though the ball could be pushed and hit by the hands, *holding* the ball with the hands was forbidden. Until this point, catching the ball with the hands was a key part of the rules followed by Cambridge University. Football historian Andy Dixon told us that without the Sheffield rules, the game we love today might look more similar to rugby, where holding the ball is allowed. Handball, ref!

LIGHTS, HEADERS, ACTION!

William Prest and Nathaniel Creswick were pioneers. The word **pioneer** was originally used for soldiers who marched ahead of their regiment to prepare the way, but is now used for people who are the first to explore new regions or introduce new ideas. And did those pals like to innovate! As well as devising a rulebook, other important elements of the game were first introduced by Sheffield FC:

Headers

In 1866, Sheffield FC played London City at an away game at Battersea Park. The London team could not stop laughing when the visitors used their heads to pass the ball to each other in the air. It was not forbidden in the rules, but it was the first time any team had used headers. This was also the first game to be played for an agreed 90 minutes.

Floodlights

Two Sheffield FC players captained the sides in the first match played under floodlights, in 1878 at Bramall Lane.

Derby match

Sheffield FC played Hallam FC on Boxing Day 1860 and the fixture, which is still played today, is football's oldest derby match.

Throw-ins, corner kicks, half-time change of ends

Thanks to Sheffield FC, the city became the national hub for football, home to about one third of the first one hundred clubs to play the game. Other Sheffield innovations included throw-ins, corner kicks and changing ends at half-time.

SHEFFIELD OF DREAMS

In order to understand why the first football club was founded in Sheffield, rather than anywhere else in Britain or the world, we need to consider how the world of work had been changing for the previous hundred years.

In the 1750s, most working people made things using their hands. But by the 1850s, a new type of workplace had emerged: the factory. One of the most important things made in factories was the metal steel, which was used for railways, ships and machines. Sheffield became the world centre of steel production. It was located in an area rich in iron ore, which is the mineral that steel is made from. In 1850, 85 per cent of the steel made in the UK was from Sheffield, and it was exported all around the world. Sheffield – nicknamed the Steel City – became rich. Its wealth and industry turned Sheffield into a centre of innovation, just the sort of place where people wanted to try a new sport.

LIGHT BULB MOMENTS

In the mid-nineteenth century, many new ideas – not just organised football – changed the world. Here are some:

DATE	INVENTION	INVENTOR
1846	Sewing machine	Elias Howe (USA)
1876	Telephone	Alexander Graham Bell (USA)
1879	Light bulb	Thomas Edison (USA)

Life without football is now just as unthinkable as life without the sewing machine, telephone and light bulb.

HOORAY FOR THE WEEKEND

Another mid-nineteenth century invention was the weekend. Before the existence of factories, people in the UK generally worked six days a week, with only Sunday off. Factory workers in places such as Sheffield, however, were allowed Saturday afternoons off too. Football was able to grow because all of a sudden people had leisure time when they could play and watch the game.

LOVE OF THE GAME

Sheffield FC was an **amateur** club, meaning that they did not pay its players. They wanted them to play only for the love of the game. In the 1880s, however, some clubs in the city became professional, meaning that their players earned money.

Sheffield FC's decision to stay amateur meant that most of their best players went to play for other teams. For example, when Sheffield United decided to start paying their players in 1889, over half of the men who turned up for the first trial were from Sheffield FC! It was not long before Sheffield FC was eclipsed by the professional teams in the city, such as Sheffield United and Sheffield Wednesday.

But while United and Wednesday might make more money and have more fans, they can never say they were the first team in Sheffield.

THAT'S YOUR LOT

Sheffield FC raised over £880,000 in 2011 after selling the original rulebook, which contained the printed *Rules, Regulations, & Laws of the Sheffield Foot-Ball Club* (as it was written then) from 1859. The buyer was anonymous. The chairman might have been hoping for a bit more money: the original document explaining the rules of basketball fetched £2.6 million at an auction in New York in 2010!

HAPPY BIRTHDAY!

Sheffield FC celebrated its 160th birthday in 2017. "Our founders created the team for the love of the game and we have worked hard to protect that," said club chairman Richard Tims. "In essence, no matter what team you support, this club is your club's great grandfather."

Today, the club has a men's side that plays in English football's eighth division, the Northern Premier League. It also fields another twenty teams across all age levels, including five women's teams. These days the women overshadow the men when it comes to success on the pitch. The women's first team was formed in 2003, starting in the bottom league. Sheffield FC Ladies kept winning and ended up with six promotions in the space of just eight seasons. In 2015, Sheffield FC Ladies beat Portsmouth 1–0 in a play-off match to reach the top division, the Women's Super League, for the first time in their history.

OLDIES BUT GOLDIES

Sheffield FC is the oldest club in the world. Here are some of the oldest clubs in other countries:

CLUB	DATE FORMED	COUNTRY
Wrexham	1864	Wales
Queen's Park	1867	Scotland
St Gallen	1879	Switzerland
Koninklijke	1879	Netherlands
Cliftonville	1879	Northern Ireland
Royal Antwerp	1880	Belgium
Hong Kong	1886	Hong Kong
North Shore United	1886	New Zealand
Germania	1888	Germany
Recreativo de Huelva	1889	Spain
Genoa	1893	Italy
Le Havre	1894	France
Rio Grande	1900	Brazil

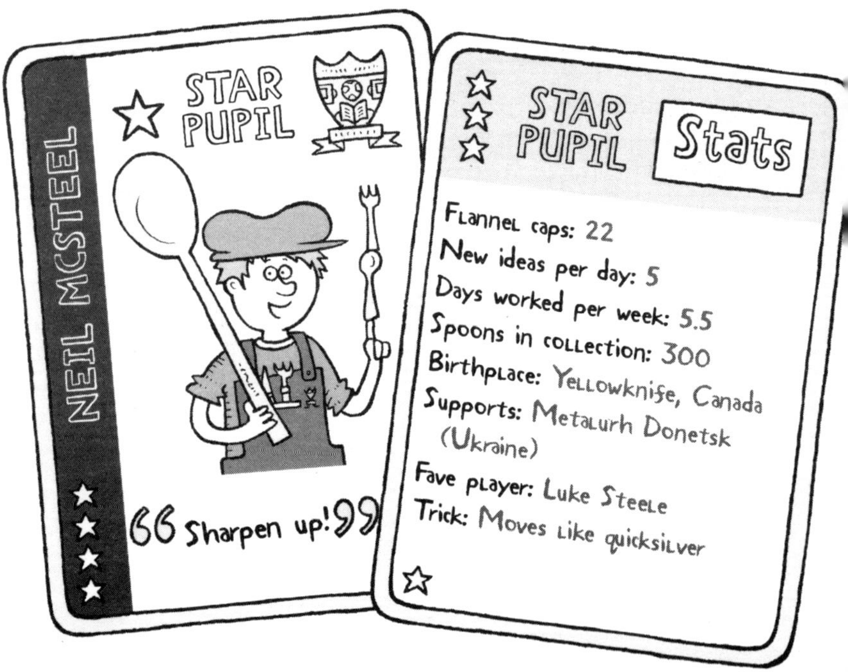

HISTORY QUIZ

1. What product was Sheffield famous for making in the 1800s?

a) Rubber
b) Brass
c) Steel
d) Gold

2. What name was given to the era from 1760–1840, in which the emergence of factories changed the world of work?

a) Factory Gold Rush
b) Industrial Revolution
c) Turbine Transformation
d) Mechanical Mutiny

3. What cutlery-related nickname are Sheffield United known by?

a) The Forks
b) The Blades
c) The Spoons
d) The Gravy Boats

4. What job did Alexander Graham Bell have when he invented the telephone?

a) Electrician
b) Monkey-trainer at Edinburgh Zoo
c) Teacher at a school for deaf children
d) Played in a travelling one-man band

5. How did Sheffield Wednesday get their name?

a) From an amateur cricket club, who only played matches on Wednesdays, then set up a football side.
b) Sheffield Tuesday never won until they played on a Wednesday, so changed their name for luck.
c) The man who founded the club was called Wilberry Wednesday.
d) Sheffield Saturday were a popular dance troupe that toured the country and Wednesday wanted to copy their success.

Thursday
Lesson 3+4

MATHS

"That's not fair!" How many times have you shouted that while watching a game? Football, like all sports, relies on fairness.

We want the rules to be applied fairly, meaning that no one side is favoured over another side. We want the players to respect the rules and show compassion and respect to the other players and fans. This is called "fair play".

But there is also another sort of fairness, which we will be talking about in this lesson. What is the "fairest" way of deciding between two teams who have shown themselves to be equal, for example by having the same amount of points in a league table?

Methods used to decide between teams include goal difference, away goals, head-to-head results and, amazingly, even the flipping of a coin. Flipping heck!

Heads or tails, anyone?

FREAKY FRACTIONS

P	W	D	L	GF	GA	PT
11	8	1	2	35	6	25
11	7	3	1	38	12	24
12	7	1	4	29	12	22
10	6	3	1	17	9	21
11	5	2	4	19	18	17
			3	21	18	16
			5	18	16	16

Alex loves looking at league tables. One reason he likes them is because the numbers are always whole numbers, such as 1, 22 and 43. Whole numbers are neat and simple.

What you never see in a league table is a **fraction**, such as 1.818 or 1.794. You need to think harder with fractions.

But Alex loves a bit of fraction action! They are to the (decimal) point!

Until about 40 years ago, every football fan was also fanatical about fractions. League tables were full of them, because back then there was a column for **goal average**, which was:

> The number of goals scored divided by the number of goals let in

So, if your team scored 60 goals at the end of the season and let in, or **conceded**, 33, they would have a goal average of:

$$60 \div 33 = 1.818$$

And if they scored 61 but conceded 34, the team would have a goal average of:

$$61 \div 34 = 1.794$$

Sounds confusing! Just think of goal average as being the number of goals you score for every goal you concede. So, a goal average of 1.794 means that, on average, you score 1.794 times for every goal you let in. Awe-sum!

$61 \div 34$

TIED UP

For almost a hundred years, goal average was the **tiebreaker** used in football leagues, meaning that if two teams were equal on points, the one with the higher goal average would be placed above the one with the lower goal average.

For example, Huddersfield Town and Cardiff City both finished the 1923–24 season at the top of the English First Division, equal on 57 points. (The First Division was the forerunner of the Premier League.)

But Huddersfield had a 1.818 goal average, compared to 1.794 for Cardiff. So Huddersfield were crowned champions by just 0.024. Eek!

Back then it paid to be good at maths if you were a football fan. In 1923, there were no electronic pocket calculators, smartphones or computers, so most people would have worked out goal average on paper using long division. Frac-attack!

DIFFERENT SYSTEM

The tiebreaker now used in the Premier League to separate two teams equal on points is **goal difference**, which is:

> The number of goals scored minus the number of goals let in

Goal difference tells you how many more goals you have scored than you have conceded. The system was introduced in the 1970s because it encourages teams to play more exciting football. We can do some sums to see why.

Imagine Alex and Ben have a team each. At the end of the season, the teams have played twenty games each and have the same number of points but the following goal records:

	GAMES PLAYED	GOALS FOR	GOALS AGAINST	GOAL AVERAGE	GOAL DIFFERENCE
TEAM ALEX	20	80	40	2	40
TEAM BEN	20	25	10	2.5	15

If we use goal average, Team Ben is better than Team Alex. But if we use goal difference, Team Alex is better than Team Ben. Who should come first in the table? Tense!

Now which team has played the most exciting football? Surely it is Team Alex, which has scored more than twice the number of goals as Team Ben. In fact, the system was changed to favour high-scoring teams, like Team Alex, over low-scoring teams, like Team Ben.

Is goal difference a fairer way to separate two teams than goal average? It depends on your point of view.

Here at Football School, we think goal difference is fairer to the fans because it encourages more goals. Defensive-minded coaches, on the other hand, may think that goal average is fairer.

Whichever one is fairest, when it comes to the calculations, goal difference is certainly easier!

BREAKOUT

Not every country uses goal difference. In Spain, the tiebreaker is the head-to-head results of the games between the two teams, and in Argentina, if the top teams have equal points, they will face a play-off. At Football School, we've come up with some great ideas for tiebreakers.

THE GREAT WORLD CUP LOTTERY

Luigi Franco Gemma was a fourteen-year-old Italian boy who took part in one of the strangest events in the history of the World Cup. In March 1954 at Rome's Olimpico stadium, he was blindfolded and asked to place his hand in a trophy cup and select one of the two pieces of paper inside.

One of the pieces of paper was marked Spain and the other Turkey. His choice would determine which of these two countries qualified for the 1954 World Cup in Switzerland.

The room was packed with the Spanish and Turkish teams and officials from FIFA. He put his hand in the cup, grabbed one of the pieces of paper, and it was … Turkey!

The Turkish delegation were overjoyed, since they were headed to the World Cup. The Spanish were devastated, since they were not.

The practice of making decisions based on putting a hand into a hat or a bowl and choosing one of several items randomly is called **drawing lots**. It is an ancient custom often used to settle disputes. The lots are the items in the selection – and this is where the word lottery comes from.

Drawing lots is seen to be the fairest way to make a choice when all other options have been exhausted, since if the choice is made randomly, then each lot has the same chance of being chosen.

Spain and Turkey had finished joint top of their World Cup qualifying group, which led to the teams playing a decider in Italy. But the game finished 2–2 after extra time, and the rules said that in the event of a draw, the winner would be decided by drawing lots.

In snatching the qualification, Turkey had lots to celebrate! They treated Luigi like a hero and even invited him to accompany the squad to the World Cup, since they thought he would bring them good luck.

For Spain, however, the result was not a-lot of fun. Even though drawing lots is part of the rules, it never feels fair to have your destiny decided by something beyond your control.

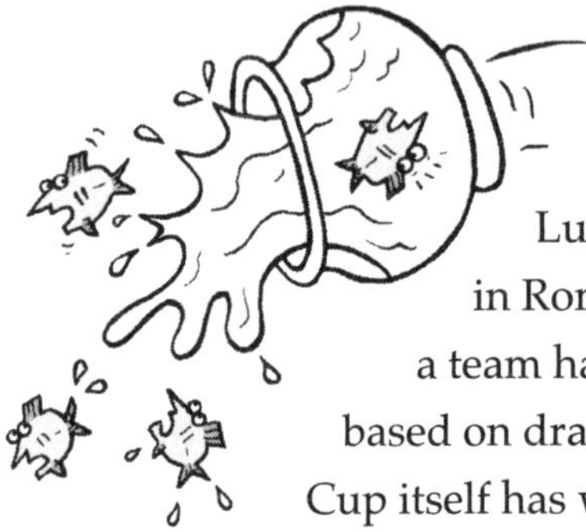

FISHY BUSINESS

Luigi Franco Gemma's fateful choice in Rome was the first and last time that a team has failed to get to the World Cup based on drawing lots. However, the World Cup itself has witnessed the drawing of lots twice since then, in 1970 and 1990.

In 1990, the tiebreakers for teams finishing equal on points in the groups stage were the following:

1990 WORLD CUP TIEBREAKERS

1) The team with the best goal difference.
2) The team that have scored most goals.
3) The winner of the match between those two teams.
4) The drawing of lots.

The tiebreakers are taken in order, so only once goal difference has been taken into account will goals scored be considered, and so on.

In 1990, Ireland and the Netherlands ended their group on the same points, the same goal difference, the same total goals scored and they had drawn the match against each other 1-1. Lots had to be drawn in order to establish which team was placed above the other.

Two yellow balls (one for Ireland and one for the Netherlands) were put in a goldfish bowl, and two red balls (with two numbers) were put in another bowl. A ball was chosen from each. The result: Ireland placed above the Netherlands.

Using lots to choose between teams may be the fairest way if all other channels have been explored, but it is never as fair as basing the decision on something that happened on the pitch. The World Cup now has an extra tiebreaker: the team's disciplinary record. In the 2018 World Cup, this method was used to separate Japan and Senegal.

The Champions League has twelve tiebreak rules for the group stages, including club coefficient, a number based on results over the previous five years. Everything is done to avoid the goldfish bowls – and the anger of fans.

THE LONG AND SHORT OF IT

Football is not the only arena where the final option is the drawing of lots. In political elections, if the two candidates with the most votes have an equal number of votes, the winner is decided by lots. This happened in the UK in a local election for Northumberland County Council in 2017. To decide the winner, the election official put a long straw and a short straw in his hand, with the same length of straw visible. The candidates had to each choose a straw, with the candidate who chose the long straw being declared the winner. That's why when we have bad luck, we often say we drew the short straw.

TOSS UP

Perhaps the most common form of drawing lots is flipping a coin, since the idea behind both is that the chances of any outcome are equal. When you flip a coin, the likelihood of it landing heads is the same as the likelihood of it landing tails.

Coins are used at the beginning of every football match. One of the team captains chooses heads or tails, the referee tosses the coin so it lands on their hand or on the ground, and the winner of the toss decides which goal his team will attack in the first half.

But did you know that coin tosses also used to happen at the end of football matches? Before the introduction of penalty shoot-outs, coin tosses were used to decide the winners of knockout matches in competitions like the European Cup, which was the top European competition before the Champions League.

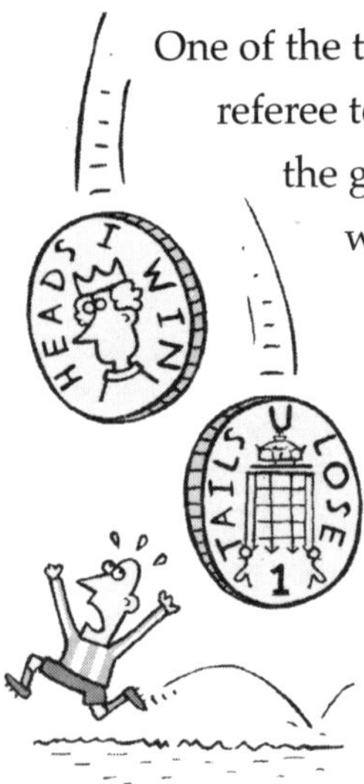

For example, in 1965, Liverpool drew 2–2 with Cologne in the quarter-finals, but the Reds qualified because they won the coin toss. In 1969, in the second round of the same competition, Celtic beat Benfica on a coin toss after their scores were 3–3 on aggregate.

The heartache for fans when these big games were decided by the flip of a coin was one of the main reasons for the introduction of the penalty shoot-out. By the end of the 1970s, penalty shoot-outs had been adopted by the European Cup, the European Championship and the World Cup. Out with the penny, in with the penalty!

ABBA-DABADOO

Using a penalty shoot-out to decide the winner requires more skill than guessing heads or tails. Yet how fair are penalty shoot-outs?

The traditional system for penalty shoot-outs is that the teams take penalties one after the other, so if the teams are A and B, the order for the first five rounds is AB AB AB AB AB. Once these five are taken, the team that has scored the most wins. If the scores are level, the teams take penalties in the same order until one scores and the other doesn't.

Ben is a penalty expert. He knows that penalties are not very fair because the team shooting first wins 60 per cent of the time on average, and the team shooting second wins only 40 per cent of the time. In other words, it's an advantage to shoot first. This is because there is more pressure on the team kicking second, especially towards the end of the shoot-out when players know that missing the penalty will lead to defeat.

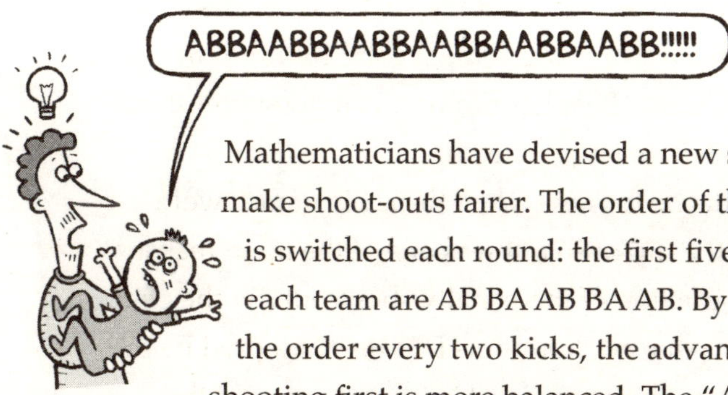

Mathematicians have devised a new system to make shoot-outs fairer. The order of the teams is switched each round: the first five kicks of each team are AB BA AB BA AB. By switching the order every two kicks, the advantage of shooting first is more balanced. The "ABBA" system may become standard in shoot-outs in the future.

COOL COINS

In ancient Rome, coins were flipped as a way of settling disputes. If the coin landed showing the face of leader Julius Caesar, it was thought that he agreed with the decision.

Around 1900, the statistician Karl Pearson flipped a coin 24,000 times in order to see what the split was between heads and tails. The result: 12,012 heads and 11,988 tails. This works out as 50.05 per cent v. 49.95 per cent.

Mathematicians in the USA investigating coin tosses built a coin-flipping machine, and estimated that a coin will land on its edge once every 6,000 throws.

MATHS QUIZ

1. **How do you calculate goal difference?**

a) Goals scored + goals let in
b) Goals scored - goals let in
c) Goals scored x goals let in
d) Goals scored ÷ goals let in

2. **What happened when referee Svein Oddvar Moen tossed a coin at the beginning of a Norwegian league game in 2015?**

a) The coin hit the head of one of the captains.
b) He flipped the coin into his own mouth.
c) He used a joke coin with two heads.
d) He is a professional magician so made the coin disappear.

3. **Which of the following are NOT used as tiebreakers in the Champions League?**

a) Away goals
b) Fair play
c) Fart average
d) Club coefficient

4. **If two coins are flipped, what is the percentage chance that both land on heads?**

a) 0 per cent
b) 25 per cent
c) 50 per cent
d) 100 per cent

5. **What did Danish assistant coach Søren Randa-Boldt say when Denmark knocked Russia out of the 2013 Women's Euros on the drawing of lots?**

a) "The Viking God Thor hammered it for us tonight!"
b) "Lady Luck smiled on the Lucky Ladies!"
c) "This was the easiest match of our lives!"
d) "I feel for Russia; it's horrible for them. But we're happy and we're ready."

Thursday
Lesson 5

GEOGRAPHY

Brrrr! Wrap up warm as we are going to one of the coldest and least populated countries in the world. Iceland is a small island almost halfway between the United Kingdom and the North Pole. It's famous all over the world for its extraordinary landscape of geographical wonders – including active volcanoes, huge waterfalls and beaches of black sand – and its millions of puffins!

Recently, the country has also become known for its extraordinary national football team, who achieved a remarkable feat. In 2018, Iceland became the smallest country in terms of population ever to play in a World Cup. In this lesson, we're going to see how these modern-day Vikings have overcome the challenges of freezing temperatures, dark nights and a small population to become a team to watch. Huuh! Huuh! Huuh!

THE LAND OF ICE, FIRE ...

Iceland is a freezing wilderness of rock, ice and fire. There are two reasons for this: a plume and two plates. The Iceland plume is a hot spot of boiling rock lying almost 2,000 miles beneath the Earth's surface, directly below Iceland. **Geologists**, the scientists who study rocks, believe Iceland was formed millions of years ago when that hot spot erupted and hot rocks, or **lava**, rose to the ocean surface, before cooling and turning into the island.

The plates are **tectonic plates**, which are huge pieces of the Earth's crust. Iceland is positioned on the border of two major tectonic plates that are moving apart at a speed of 2.5 centimetres per year. It doesn't sound much but that's over 15 miles every million years. As the plates move apart, they cause openings for molten rock to burst through. Mountains created by the lava that spurts out are called **volcanoes**. Iceland has 130 volcanoes, and one of them will erupt approximately once every four years.

When Iceland's volcanoes erupt, the rest of the world knows about it. One eruption in 2010 released a huge cloud of ash that made it impossible for planes to fly across Europe. Thousands of flights were cancelled and

millions of passengers were stranded. One cancelled flight was booked by Barcelona for their Champions League semi-final tie against Inter Milan. As they couldn't fly to Italy, Barcelona travelled the 600 miles by bus instead. They were tired when they arrived in Italy and they lost the game 3-1. What a pa-LAVA!

Iceland's volcanic activity also means there are bubbling pools of hot water or vents of steam, known as **geysers**, all over the country. Iceland's capital, Reykjavik, translates as Smoky Bay, a name that dates from the time Viking settlers arrived more than a thousand years ago and found hot springs that produced steam. Some of these hot springs are the temperature of a warm bath, so despite the cold you can have an outdoor soak all year round. Don't forget your towels!

But Iceland is not named after its hot parts. Ten per cent of the country is covered by **glaciers**, which are vast sheets of slow-moving ice. Glaciers are formed over many years, when snow doesn't melt but turns to ice. The ice sheets are constantly moving under their own weight. Freezy does it!

... AND FAKE GRASS

Being so far north means the days in Iceland vary dramatically in length. In the summer, it only gets dark for a few hours each night. But in the winter, it is light for just a few hours a day. In the middle of December in Reykjavik, for example, the sun rises after 11am and sets around 3pm. The dark, along with the snow and ice, make it difficult to play football outdoors in Iceland all year round.

To solve this problem, the Icelandic FA came up with a plan to build as many indoor artificial pitches as possible. There are now almost 150 indoor arenas, which are heated and well-lit so the weather and darkness can't stop play. "There is now an artificial pitch close to almost every school in Iceland," said the national team coach Heimir Hallgrimsson. There are also over 600 UEFA-qualified coaches, who work on improving children's technique from the age of three upwards. That translates to one coach to every 550 Icelanders, compared to England's one per 11,000. Good facilities + good coaches = good skills!

SMALL YET STRONG

Perhaps the greatest challenge to Iceland having a good national team is the number of Icelanders.

The USA has a population of about 327 million, Brazil has about 210 million, England has 53 million and Scotland has 5 million. Yet Iceland's population is only 340,000 – about the size of a medium-sized city such as Reading or Coventry.

In fact, the entire population of Iceland is equivalent to only four full Wembley stadiums!

How on earth do you get a team good enough to qualify for the World Cup from such a small pool of talent? Our mate Kristján Jónsson, a football writer based in Reykjavik, says it's down to several reasons:

- Icelanders are descended from the Vikings and come from generations of fisherman and farmers. Growing up doing physical work in harsh weather conditions encourages a tough attitude to life.

- The Iceland players have all played alongside each other since they were young, so they know each other very well. That team spirit is a big advantage.

- Icelanders understand the value of teamwork. In a small community no one likes a show-off! "You can't act like you're better than anyone else," says Kristján.

- The small size of the island means community is strong. Everyone knows each other. The team celebrate with the fans because they are fans too.

THE ICE MEN COMETH ... MEET THE TEAM

Here is the inside scoop on the team that brought Iceland to the 2018 World Cup: it's a story of kicks, cameras, teeth and tenacity.

THE FREE KICK EXPERT

Gylfi Sigurdsson is Iceland's most famous player. He has played in the Premier League for Tottenham Hotspur, Swansea and Everton, and is known as one of the best free kick takers in the world. He has won Icelandic Player of the Year for six years in a row. Sigurdsson's older brother Olafur helped improve his technique from the age of five, and his dad once rented a warehouse in the winter so the pair always had somewhere to play. Practice really does make perfect!

THE FILM-MAKER

Playing football in Iceland is only a part-time job, which means that some players need another job to earn money when they are not on the pitch. Goalkeeper Hannes Thor Halldorsson makes films: he made his first when he was twelve years old. Since then, he has directed Iceland's music video for the 2012 Eurovision Song Contest (it was about an elf and Iceland finished twentieth) and a video for Iceland's national airline, which starred his teammates – and himself! He also worked on a horror film that he described as a "supernatural ghost thriller that takes place in an isolated part of Iceland". Spooky!

THE DENTIST

Heimir Hallgrimsson combined his role as Iceland national team coach at the 2018 World Cup with his other job as a professional dentist in his hometown of Heimaey. Seeing his patients allowed him to take his mind off football for a while. And calming his patients' nerves before they go into his dentist chair helped him practise telling the players not to be nervous before games. "As a dentist, you have to treat a patient who might be scared," he said. "Probably it's the same with players, you speak to them in different ways too..." And if he loses his coaching job, he knows what he will do next. Open wide and say "Aaah!"

THE FANS

Heimir Hallgrimsson is unique in world football for another reason. Many teams call their fans the twelfth man, but the relationship between Iceland fans and their team is closer than most. When he was assistant coach, Hallgrimsson used to meet fans before matches to explain the line-up and tactics. "It's something that makes us different and I really believe it has strengthened the connection between the supporters and the team," Hallgrimsson explained. He did the same even when he was head coach. "I see going to the pub with the fans and then meeting the team at the stadium as my pre-match routine now." Imagine Pep Guardiola or José Mourinho doing the same!

THUNDERING SUCCESS

This connection remains strong after matches, when Iceland players approach the fans and perform a ritual "Thunderclap". The players raise their arms out wide and, starting slowly, do a single clap over their heads. As their hands connect, they shout, "Huuh!" The fans copy them. Gradually, the speed and volume of the clapping and chanting increases and rises to a thunderous crescendo. Give those fans a big hand!

Some people thought the chant went back to ancient times when the inhabitants of Iceland were Vikings, but the truth is not quite so exciting. Twenty-two fans of one Icelandic club Stjarnan went to watch their team play Scottish side Motherwell in a 2014 European game. Motherwell fans performed a version of the Thunderclap that the Stjarnan fans took home with them. The Iceland team's fans liked it so much that they adopted it with their own players. The volume of the clap and bond it helps create between fans and players is the envy of teams worldwide.

ICE QUEENS

Icelanders believe that women and men should be given the same opportunities in life. At Football School, we agree! Iceland recently came first in a survey ranking gender equality across the world. So it's no surprise that Iceland's women's team is also incredibly successful. They reached the European championship quarter-finals in 1994 and 2013 and, in 2017, became the first team to beat Germany in a World Cup qualifying match for nineteen years.

THE NAME GAME

Icelanders don't have family names. Instead men usually use the names of their fathers appended with *-son*, meaning son, and women use the names of their fathers, appended with *-dóttir*, meaning daughter. For example, Gylfi Sigurdsson is so called because he is the son of Sigurd. The all-time leading scorer for the Iceland women's team, Margrét Lára Vidarsdóttir, is so called because she is the daughter of Vidar. Some people use their mother's names, like former Icelandic forward Heidar Helguson, son of Helga. Alex and Ben's Icelandic names would be Alex Davidsson (father's name) and Ben Andreuson (mother's name). What's yours?

ELF AND SAFETY

The majority of people in Iceland believe that the country is also home to an invisible tribe of elves called Huldufólk, meaning the hidden people. Construction work on a road in Reykjavik was stopped when campaigners warned it would disrupt elves living in a 12-foot rock which believers call the Elf Chapel. "You can't live in this landscape and not believe in a force greater than you," said Adalheidur Gudmundsdottir, a Professor of Folklore at the University of Iceland.

GEOGRAPHY QUIZ

1. What does Iceland's capital city Reykjavik translate to in the local language?

a) Land of Puffins
b) Home to Volcanoes
c) Smoky Bay
d) Bring extra socks

2. Which of the following letters are not in the Icelandic alphabet?

a) O, M, G
b) C, Q, W
c) G, O, L
d) X, Y, Z

3. Which of the following is the only one you can find in Iceland:

a) Motorways
b) McDonald's restaurants
c) Mosquitoes
d) Ice cream

4. What was special about Vigdís Finnbogadóttir, who served as Iceland's President from 1980–96?

a) Her previous job was coach of the Iceland women's football team.
b) She was the world's first elected female president.
c) She played in goal for Iceland while serving as president.
d) She was a famous pop star.

5. Iceland forward Eidur Gudjohnsen won two Premier League titles with Chelsea and the Champions League with Barcelona. Why was his Iceland debut, aged 17, a family occasion?

a) His uncle was Iceland coach at the time.
b) He came on as a substitute and replaced his dad.
c) His brother was playing for the opposition.
d) His grandfather was in goal.

Friday
Lesson 1+2

CHEMISTRY

This lesson will be more exciting than watching paint dry.

Actually, this lesson is going to be about watching paint dry!

Paint is a colourful subject. It is a fascinating and important material, and the world depends on it. Look around you and you will see paint: in your room on the walls, the door, the ceiling and the window frames; outside on cars, signs, roads, buildings, planes, trains, ships and more.

When you are watching a game of football, you are also watching paint: the bright white lines that mark the boundary of the pitch, the boxes and the centre circle.

In this lesson, we will find out about what goes into paint, why it is like cake (yes, you read that right) and how it is applied on the grass of a pitch.

Let's paint the town red! No, we mean the grass white!

THE WHITE STUFF

In football's distant past, pitches were often marked out using … weedkiller!

Weedkiller left ugly yellow lines of dead grass. Horrible! Grounds teams also used paint made from a white powder called lime, but lime sometimes burnt players' skin.

These nasty substances aren't used any more. Pitches are now marked using brilliant white paint that allows the grass to live and players to avoid rashes. A-grazing!

There have been many other advances in paint technology since the bad old grass-murdering and skin-burning days, but before we get there, put on your chefs' hats and aprons, because we are going into the kitchen.

GREAT CHEMISTRY

The study of how substances interact with each other is called **chemistry**. But did you know that all baking is chemistry? When we bake a cake, the different ingredients we put in the mixing bowl interact with each other to eventually become cake.

At Football School, we love eating cake. (Especially Ben!) We also love cake because it explains to us how paint works. Yes, paint is just like cake. We don't mean that you can eat paint or stick candles in it. Warning! Please do not eat paint!

But let's look at how the chemistry of paint is just like the chemistry of cake. On your marks. Get Set. Bake!

MAGIC SPONGE CAKE

To make a cake you must assemble various ingredients, mix them together, and then bake the mix in the oven. When it comes out, the mix has turned into a solid cake. It tastes and smells delicious. Here's Ben's favourite recipe for cake:

BEN'S CAKE OF CHAMPIONS

INGREDIENTS	METHOD
Eggs	1. Create mixture.
Flour	(Assemble ingredients and put
Butter	in a bowl and mix.)
Sugar	2. Apply mixture to desired
Nuts	location. (Pour it in a cake tin.)
Raisins	3. Mixture undergoes a chemical
Dates	change. (Bake it in the oven.)
Carrots	

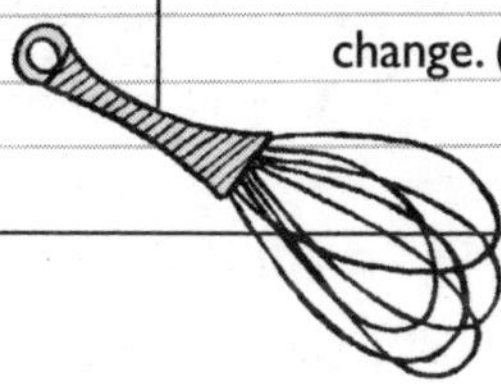

As the mixture turns into cake, each of the ingredients plays a role. The eggs, flour, butter and sugar make the sponge. The nuts, raisins and dates give the cake flavour. The carrot fills out the cake and gives it texture.

The most important part of the cake is the sponge, since the sponge binds everything together. If there was no sponge, there would be no cake. Once the mixture is put in the oven, the heat causes chemical changes to take place and the gooey mess solidifies into the finished cake. Yum!

PLAYED A BINDER

Now let's think about how paint works. Fresh paint comes in tins. You open the tin, dip a brush in it, brush the paint on a surface and then wait for it to dry. The process is the same as baking a cake, but this time the main ingredients are not food but chemicals we call **binder**, **pigment** and **filler**:

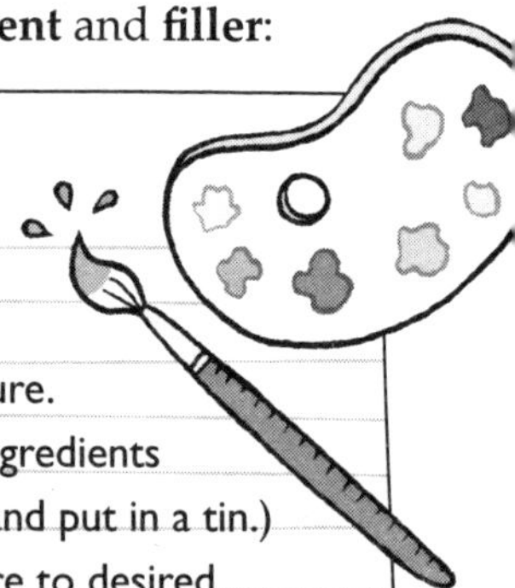

PAINT

INGREDIENTS	METHOD
Binder Pigment Filler	1. Create mixture. (Assemble ingredients in a factory and put in a tin.) 2. Apply mixture to desired location. (Brush or spray paint on a surface.) 3. Mixture undergoes a chemical change. (Leave to dry.)

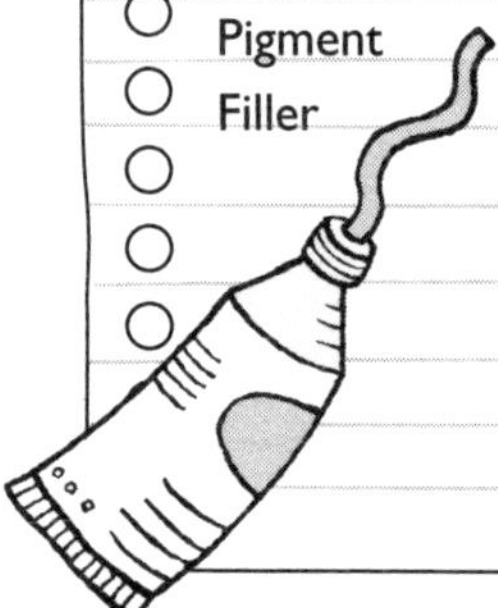

The chemical ingredients do different things. The binder is a transparent substance that is only there to bind all the other ingredients together. (It's like the sponge in the cake.)

The pigment is the substance in the paint that provides the colour. (Just like the nuts and raisins add flavour.)

The filler fills out the paint and may change the texture. (Just like the carrot.)

Paint starts off as a liquid and undergoes a chemical change, ending up as a solid layer of colour. The process of paint drying is so similar to the process of cake baking that chemists consider "drying" a type of baking that happens at room temperature. Those crazy chemists!

FANS' FAVOURITE FANCIES

ALL IN THE MIX

By tweaking a cake's ingredients, you can change its characteristics, for example, making it fluffier, denser or more moist. Likewise, by tweaking the three ingredients of paint, you can change its characteristics. Paint is used for many things and each of them has different requirements. Look at these examples:

For pitch markings:

1) Must be visible from a long way away
2) Must not kill the grass
3) Must be waterproof
4) Must look good for a week or so, but doesn't have to last longer than that

For stadium walls:

1) Must last for years as you don't want to paint them every week
2) Must be waterproof since they will be rained on
3) Must be tough as will get scuffed by fans walking next to them

For your bedroom:

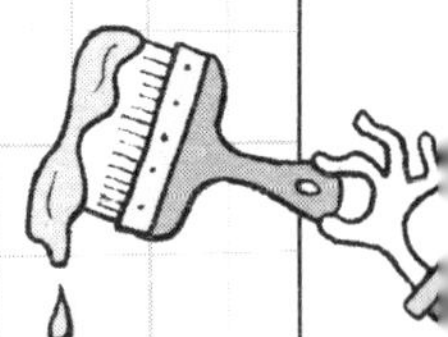

1) Must last for years
2) Must look good in lots of colours
3) Does not need to be waterproof, since it doesn't rain indoors
4) Must be resistant to cleaning with a cloth as you might spill something on it

THIS LITTLE PIGMENT

When you watch a football match, you may or may not be watching players who come from far away countries. But you will definitely be watching paint that does – most probably Australia, South Africa, Canada or Mozambique.

This is because the white pigment used in white paint is the chemical titanium dioxide, which you get from **ilmenite**, a substance found in sand and rock. The biggest sources of ilmenite in the world are Australia, South Africa, Canada and Mozambique. Rock on!

PITCH PERFECT

When a film star gets ready for a photo shoot, they will get their hair and make-up done. The same thing happens when a professional football pitch gets ready for a game. But for hair, read grass, and for make-up, read paint. The idea in both cases is to look as attractive as possible.

At about 8am on a match day, the grounds team will give the pitch a trim by mowing it. This takes a couple of hours. Then it's time to prepare it for painting. The first step is to "string out" the pitch, meaning that pegs are placed at the ends of the lines that will be painted, and the string pulled taut along the lines. The string acts as a reference so that when the lines are painted, they go in a straight line.

Small and amateur clubs tend to use painting machines that look like a golf trolley with three wheels. Paint pours onto the middle wheel, which marks the line on the grass as the wheel rolls along. Since the wheel rolls the grass stems flat, only one side of the stem is painted, so the line has to be repainted in the other direction too. Then the line is wheelie-good!

Top clubs now use machines with spray paint: the paint is blown out of a tiny nozzle as a fine mist. This method does not flatten the stems and the paint gets on both sides in one spray, meaning that you only need to paint the line once. The paint mist also means that only a very thin layer of paint gets on the grass. In fact, it is possible to use only 1 litre of paint to mark up an entire pitch, although clubs will use around 10 litres so the white is as bright as possible.

Once the pitch is painted – the whole process, including stringing out, takes about an hour and a half – it is left to dry. Spray paint dries in about 20 minutes, but wheeled-out paint needs longer. Once the paint is dry, the string is removed, so it doesn't trip up the players when they come on the pitch. No one wants to be tackled by a piece of string! Once dry, the pitch is watered and left for a couple of hours before the players warm up.

RAIN, RAIN GO AWAY

The biggest enemy of pitch paint is the rain! If it's bucketing down, you get problems. Paint applied on the wet grass will mix with the water and become thinner, so the white will be less bright. Watery paint won't stick to the stems, so it will run off into the soil. Rain also means the paint doesn't dry as quickly and, in some cases, it will rub off onto the players. One groundsman we spoke to said that once his lines didn't dry in time and when the goalkeeper dived, he ended up with white shirt and white hair. "He aged forty years in ninety minutes!" he said. The grounds team are always checking the weather forecast and hoping match days are dry. They may even paint the lines the night before if it means dodging a shower.

GOLD TRAFFORD

Football clubs are always blaming bad results on referees. But top Chinese team Guangzhou R&F once blamed the paint. Guangzhou play in blue and their stadium used to be blue. But after a run of bad results, the club decided to repaint the entire stadium gold. And it seemed to work. When it was blue, they had only one home win in four months, but when the stadium was gold, they then won their next five games on the trot. Goooaaald!

CHEMISTRY QUIZ

1. What is the name of the substance that gives paint colour?

a) Piglet
b) Pigtail
c) Pigeon
d) Pigment

2. What is the total length of the white lines that must be painted around the Wembley pitch, which is 105m long and 69m wide?

a) 174m
b) 243m
c) 348m
d) 420m

3. What is a common filler for paint?

a) Socks
b) Chalk
c) Cheese
d) Carrot

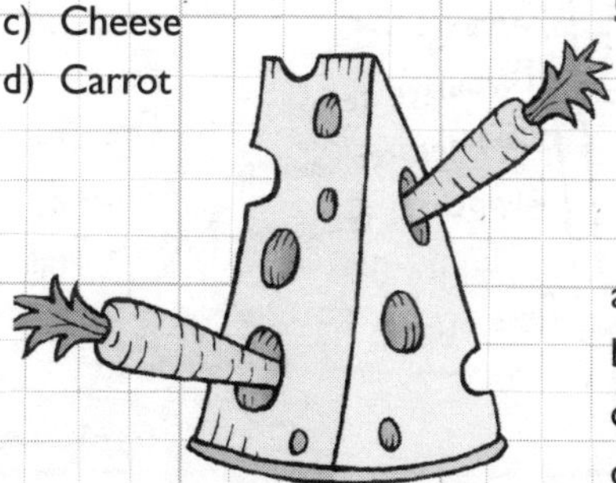

4. What paint nightmare happened during a game in 2016 between MLS rivals Montreal Impact and Toronto?

a) The match was delayed by 30 minutes as the grounds team repainted the penalty box lines.
b) It started to rain hard, wiping off the paint marks and leaving the linesmen unable to tell if a ball was in or out.
c) The paint hadn't dried in time and, by the end of the game, footprints could be seen all over the pitch.
d) The club ran out of white paint halfway through painting, so the penalty boxes were painted in red.

5. Titanium dioxide is a chemical used in white paint that is made up of atoms of titanium and which other substance?

a) Hydrogen
b) Oxygen
c) Oxtail
d) Oxlade-Chamberlain

Friday
Lesson 3+4
FASHION
What do you call two quick breaths?
Huh? Huh?
AB
BL
A pair of pants!
That joke is pants!
BL
What's soft and slippery?
A slipper!
Toe-tally bad...
BL

People are always changing their clothes.

That's to say, people are always changing their minds about clothes. Alex used to love wearing flip-flops, but now he always wears trainers. Ben used to love his stripy pyjamas, but now he prefers the ones with polka dots. Why do we change our minds about what we wear? Surely as long as our clothes keep us warm and are comfortable, it shouldn't matter how they look.

But we've all had a moment where we've wanted a piece of clothing that is new and different to what's in our wardrobes. In this lesson, we're going to learn about fashion and football kits. We'll admire some classic shirt designs and snigger at some hideous ones.

Looking good!

AFTER A FASHION

We change our opinions about the clothes we wear for many reasons, such as when we:

- See something we like online, in a magazine, on TV or in a shop
- Get bored with what we are wearing and want something new
- See a friend wearing something cool and want it too

We say an item of clothing is **in fashion** if it is very popular, and **out of fashion** (like Alex's old flip-flops) if it is unpopular. Clothes can go in and out of fashion very quickly. One day, everyone in class might be wearing red socks and then, a few weeks later, no one will be seen dead in red socks. These fashion moments, when everyone copies the same look, are called **trends**.

No single person decides what will be in fashion. Rather, it depends on many factors, such as what's on TV, what's in the shops, how much money we have, what celebrities (including footballers) are wearing, what new fabrics scientists have invented or even what the weather is like.

TRENDSETTERS

Clothes companies try to create fashions in order to sell more clothes, but this doesn't always work. Fashion and trends can be hard to predict.

One reason things go in and out of fashion is human psychology. We like to feel that we fit in with our friends, and wearing the same clothes as them is an obvious way to show to the world that we think the same things are important. This is why people love to wear band T-shirts or the kit of their favourite team. Fashion can make you feel like you belong in a group.

But we also like to stand out and show people we are different and special. It's a delicate balance. No one wants to look like they've just copied their mate or a celebrity. Often when an item of clothing becomes too popular, people stop wearing it, since wearing something everyone else is wearing shows a lack of individuality.

Fashion is like a big wheel, with things always coming into fashion, going out of fashion and then coming back into fashion. One day, Alex may even wear his flip-flops again!

FASHION VICTIMS

Footballers are not afraid to try new fashions. Here are some we applaud for trying to stand out:

Dani Alves

The Brazilian loves brightness in his fashion choices, from gold trainers with teddy bears on the tongue to shiny jackets with artistic prints. Our favourite outfit of Dani's came before a Champions League tie in 2015: a red tuxedo, black bow tie, black shorts and rhinestone-encrusted suede loafers with the image of Batman's The Joker on them. No wonder he moved to the home of fashion, Paris, in 2017!

Mario Balotelli

When asked who his most stylish teammate was, the Italian replied, "Me." He specialises in eccentric headgear, from the hoodie with its own Mohawk, to the "glove hat", a brown-and-yellow woollen beanie with five fingers sticking up along the top of his head.

David Beckham

The former England captain wore a sarong over a pair of black trousers during the 1998 World Cup. He did not regret it, even if people at the time joked: "How can anything that seems so right be sarong?"

Megan Rapinoe

The American midfielder set up her own clothing brand with twin sister Rachael to help people stand up for what they believe in. Rapinoe supports women's rights, LGBTQ rights and racial justice, and her clothes have messages that sum up her approach to life: be authentic and help others do the same. One of her T-shirts says: Be your best you!

THE KIT CATWALK

Football kits are a brilliant way of seeing how trends keep changing, and often come full circle. Sometimes shirts with collars are in fashion, sometimes V-necks are all the rage and at other times crew necks are the style. Sometimes shorts only just cover players' bums and at other times they reach down to their knees.

Clubs like updating their kits every year for many reasons. A new, exciting kit design makes players look and feel special, promising a glorious future. (Don't you always feel good when you put on a brand new shirt?) A new kit also means the club can sell more replica shirts, since fans always want to have the latest item. But kit designs are also responding to wider changes in society. Here we'll see that the introduction of floodlights, the invention of new fabrics and the rise of the European Cup (now what we call the Champions League) are all things that have changed what footballers wear.

A SHORT HISTORY OF FOOTBALL STRIPS

1900S TO 1930S: KNEESY DOES IT

At the beginning of the last century, tight-fitting shirts with vertical stripes were the big trend. They had long sleeves and were usually made from heavyweight cotton. The most popular style was a crew neck (a rounded neckline) with laces. A rule requiring players to cover their knees was abolished, so for the first time in football history, knees were on show – and shorts reached to just above them. Knee-t! The dyes used for clothes at that time were not colour-fast, so football shirts would look more and more washed-out as the season went on.

Women's football became popular during the First World War. Sometimes women wore the same kit as the men, but sometimes they wore very different kits that included full or calf-length skirts. They used bonnets in the team colours to keep their hair up.

1930S TO 1950S: BUTTONS UP

The first World Cup was played in 1930, by which time no one wanted a crew neck anymore. The most common shirt style in the UK had a collar and buttons down the front. Below the waist, shorts became baggy and there was a trend for hoops around the socks. Hoop hoop, hooray!

1950s: LIGHTWEIGHT

A few years after the end of the Second World War, which lasted between 1939 and 1945, English and Scottish clubs started to play against European clubs in tournaments such as the European Cup. Many of these European teams were better than the British clubs, and they wore a much more lightweight kit. As a result, the Brits copied their look. Out went the heavy collars and baggy shorts, and in came slick V-necks, short sleeves and shorter shorts. Heavy woollen socks became a thing of the past, and were replaced by lightweight nylon ones.

1960s: BRIGHT WHITE

The 1960s was a period of great cultural change and artistic creativity. New pop bands like The Beatles wore clothes that were neat and unfussy, and this was reflected in football. Shirts now had basic crew necks and long sleeves. The introduction of floodlights led to several clubs, most famously Leeds United, adopting all-white strips – white shirts, shorts and socks – which stood out particularly well.

1970S: FLARE FOR FASHION

If you look at photos of bands from the 1970s, you will see big haircuts, bold colours, glitter and flared trousers. Football fashion embraced this sense of excess. In England, shirts featured long droopy collars and decorative stripes down the side of the arms. And the hair! England's best player Kevin Keegan became as famous for his "poodle" haircut as for his skills.

1980S: MATERIAL MANIA

New materials and manufacturing techniques radically changed the look and feel of football shirts. Artificial fabrics like polyester were much lighter to wear than the traditional cotton, and didn't get heavy with sweat. It was also possible to produce very intricate designs like pinstripes and shadow stripes. The V-neck style was favoured. Players were allowed to choose whether to wear long or short sleeves, except at Arsenal where it was the captain's decision.

1990S: OFF-PITCH STYLE

At the end of the twentieth century, it became fashionable for fans to buy replica shirts and wear them to matches. Then fans started to wear the replica kit all the time, at home and when out with friends. As a result, clubs started to design football shirts made to look good with jeans. This period was the most creative time for shirt designers. They introduced lots of new colours, such as powder blue and silver grey, and designed many inventive patterns, such as splotches, wavy stripes and even tiger stripes.

The first Women's World Cup was held in 1991, and the women's game became more popular throughout the decade. Women's kit in general has the same style as the men's.

2000 TO NOW: SKIN TIGHT

The crazy designs of the previous decade settled down and the styles became much simpler again. What is seen as important now is less the pattern on the shirt but making sure the latest advances in fabric technology makes them as light and as water resistant as possible. Shorts became really long and baggy – at one point down to the knees, a length not seen for a hundred years – but are now rising again. Another innovation by some shirt manufacturers was to use super-skinny designs that look like they have been shrink-wrapped.

FOOTBALL SCHOOL'S WARDROBE OF WACKINESS

Welcome to our collection of curious and interesting shirts from around the world. Most teams prefer plain colours, stripes or hoops. But not all…

Croatia

Check them out! Also doubles as a draughts board.

Hull City

In 1992, the Tigers roared with these stripes.

Netherlands

In 1988, the Dutch were unparalleled in their use of parallelograms.

Peru

The Peruvians love to sashay with a sash.

Arsenal

In 1991, Arsenal's yellow away kit was nicknamed the "bruised banana".

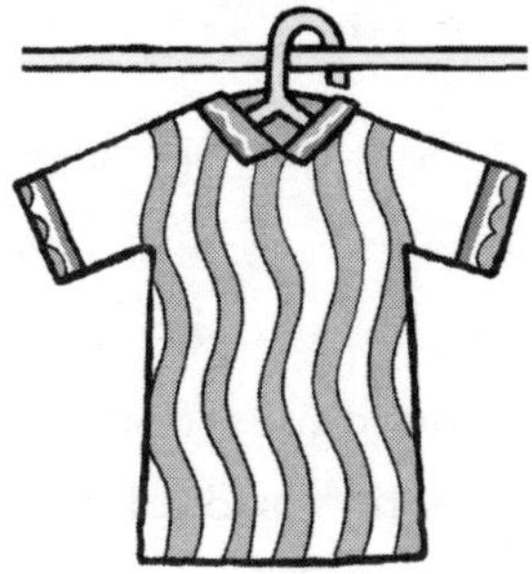

USA

Painted by hand? No, USA's 1994 World Cup kit had wobbly stripes.

Mexico

Based on the Aztec calendar, this 1998 World Cup shirt knows what day it is.

Cultural Leonesa

In 2014, the second division Spanish side donned a suit and bow tie. Champagne for all!

Chicago Red Stars

We award this team from USA's National Women's Soccer League four stars!

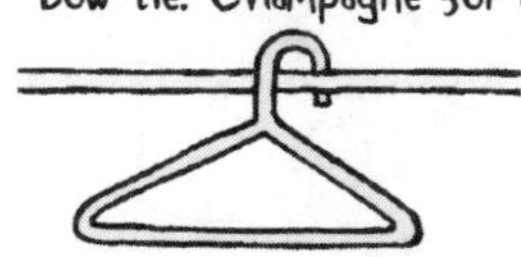

STRIPS WITH STRIPES

A shirt with vertical stripes makes you look thinner and taller. A shirt with horizontal stripes, known as hoops, makes you look shorter and wider. This optical illusion is one reason why vertical stripes are much more common than hoops in football, but hoops are much more common than vertical stripes in rugby. Footballers like to look tall, but rugby players want to look as bulky as possible.

FASHION QUIZ

1. Which part of the footballer's body was exposed during matches for the first time at the beginning of the twentieth century?

a) The neck
b) The belly button
c) The bum
d) The knees

2. British kit-maker Humphreys Brothers later changed its name to which well-known sports brand?

a) Umbro
b) Adidas
c) Nike
d) Puma

3. Which of the following words means the same as "unfashionable"?

a) Groovy
b) Passé
c) Chic
d) Hot

4. Which European football club has sold the most replica shirts over the last decade?

a) Barcelona
b) Real Madrid
c) Bayern Munich
d) Manchester United

5. A football shirt is sometimes called a jersey, the name coming from the island of Jersey in the English Channel. Why?

a) The ancient inhabitants of Jersey were brilliant footballers.
b) Footballers used to wear protective leather tops made from the skin of Jersey cows.

c) Jersey's sailors were famous for their woolly jumpers.
d) The people of Jersey were the first to stitch numbers onto the back of their clothes.

Friday
Lesson 5

DESIGN AND TECHNOLOGY

It only happens a few times every year and it's one of the most memorable, most photographed and symbolic sights in football: the moment when the team captain lifts the trophy to celebrate a victory.

In this lesson, we're going to ask why we use trophies to celebrate a win and also discover more about the materials they're made from. We will meet the oldest trophy in football and try to solve three trophy mysteries that have baffled the world.

Hands up if you're ready to lift the cup!

LEAFY DOES IT

Your team has won the final. The glory is yours. Surely that's all you need?

Not quite. It is human nature to also want a prize that you can look at and touch. This prize will be a constant reminder to you – and your rivals! – of your triumph. In nearly all sports, the winner of a tournament receives an object, known as a trophy, which reminds them of their moment of glory long after the event. Trophies are traditionally objects such as a cup, statuette, medal and dish – or, in the case of Spanish bullfighting, one or two of the bull's ears. Oh ear-ie me!

Trophies have been part of sporting events for thousands of years. In the ancient Olympic Games, the world's earliest major sporting tournament held from around 800 BC, victorious athletes were crowned with a wreath of olive leaves cut from a sacred tree. Other Greek games gave crowns of celery leaves, pine leaves and bay leaves. (Bay is also known as laurel, which is where the phrase "to rest on one's laurels" comes from, meaning to make no further effort because one has already achieved enough.)

Nowadays, trophies are usually made out of metal and, in the case of football, often shaped like a cup. Historians have long tried to get a handle (or two) on why a receptacle for drink became a symbol for sporting success, but the reason is not entirely clear. The first cups – wine goblets – began to appear as sporting trophies in the seventeenth century. By the time football became a popular sport two hundred years later, the idea of cups as trophies was an established part of sporting culture. Up the cups!

GOLD RUSH

The two most popular materials for trophies are gold and silver. These precious metals have long been associated with wealth. The reasons gold and silver are considered valuable are:

- They are both quite rare. You could fit every piece of gold ever mined in the world into a square box with 20-metre sides.
- They are lustrous. Most metals are grey or silvery grey, so gold and silver stand out and look pretty.
- They are long-lasting. More common metals tend to tarnish. Copper goes green and iron goes red when exposed to air and water, but gold and silver stay shiny for longer.

SOFT TOUCH

Compared to other metals, gold and silver are both quite soft and **malleable**, meaning they easily bend. When gold or silver is used to make a trophy, the precious metal is usually mixed with other metals to make it harder and stronger. A material made from lots of metals is called an **alloy**.

The most common material used in making trophies is sterling silver, which is made of 92.5 per cent pure silver. The remaining 7.5 per cent is other metals, mainly copper. Sterling silver is tough, and harder to scratch or damage than pure silver.

To make a gold trophy, pure gold is mixed with metals such as silver, copper and zinc. Gold purity is measured using **carats**, a word that comes not from carrots but from the carob tree, whose seeds were used as weights when measuring out gold. Pure gold is 24 carats. The World Cup trophy is 18-carat gold, which means it is 75 per cent pure gold. That's enough gold to make it glisten, but tough enough to withstand a trophy celebration!

Because gold is so soft, it can be hammered into paper-thin sheets. Sometimes trophies are made of a material called silver gilt, which is silver covered with a thin layer of gold.

TROPHY		LOOKS LIKE	MATERIAL
World Cup		Two figures holding the globe	18-carat gold
Champions League	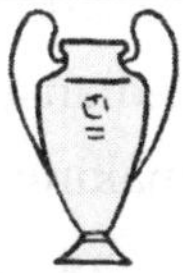	Your aunt's favourite vase with big handles	Sterling silver
Women's Champions League		Vase with ribbon sash	Sterling silver
Serie A		Giant toothpaste tube with funnel on top	Blue sodalite and silver gilt
Premier League	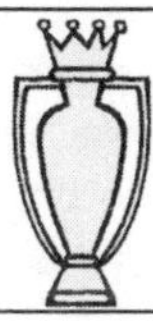	Crown atop giant vase	Sterling silver
Bundesliga	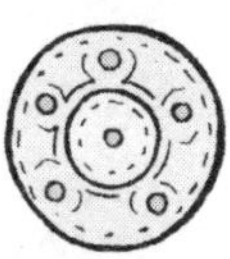	Poshest fruit bowl ever	Sterling silver
Ligue 1	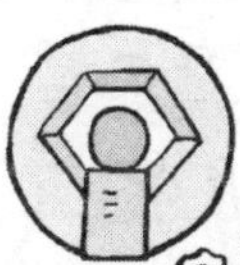	Old vinyl record with a football in the middle	Plexiglass, aluminium and resin

A DAY IN THE LIFE OF FOOTBALL'S OLDEST TROPHY

The oldest football trophy in existence is the Scottish Football Association Challenge Cup. It has been presented to the winners of the Scottish FA Cup since the 1873–4 season. With the help of the Scottish Football Museum's curator, the cup spoke exclusively to Football School.

I'm made of silver and almost 150 years old. I live in a glass cabinet at the Scottish Football Museum at Hampden Park stadium in Glasgow. I get scrubbed twice a year and I've been cleaned so often that I've probably lost about half my original silver. It's an exciting life being the world's oldest football trophy!

I need to glisten on the day of the Scottish FA Cup final. It's my day of glory! Richard McBrearty, the museum curator, picks me up wearing white cotton gloves. I am guest of honour at a lunch for the two clubs in the final. The guests gaze at me in awe. I look at them and pray they don't spill anything near me!

Richard moves me to an office and never takes his eyes off me during the game. True love! As soon as the final whistle blows, an engraver carves the winning team's name on a silver plaque on my plinth. (That's the wooden bit I stand on.) Then Richard whisks me off into the sunshine!

I am handed to the captain of the winning team. By now, Richard is looking very anxious because he is no longer able to protect me. Chill out, Dickie! This is my moment! The stadium roars as the captain lifts me above his head. Then the team take me onto the pitch for a lap of honour. Easy does it, boys! The players know to be careful – and the fans go crazy when they see me!

When the team leaves the pitch, Richard is there. He gives them a replica cup, which looks just like me, and he is almost tearful with relief when he holds me again. Then I'm back in my cabinet, exhausted. What a magic afternoon!

FOOTBALL SCHOOL LIBRARY

THE WORLD CUP TROPHY MYSTERIES

The original World Cup trophy, given to the winners of the World Cup from 1930 to 1970, has one of the most baffling histories in football. It was the centre of THREE separate mysteries and still to this day has not been found. Let's open the casebook and see if you can succeed where the world's best sleuths have failed.

Mystery 1: The Rimet Riddle

Frenchman Jules Rimet planned the World Cup. He asked Abel Laffleur, a sculptor from Paris, to design a trophy for the first competition in 1930. Laffleur made a silver trophy of a cup being supported by Nike, the Greek goddess of victory, and coated it with gold. It was later renamed the Jules Rimet trophy.

Experts believe something happened to the Jules Rimet trophy between 1954 and 1958. The trophy Brazil won in Sweden in 1958 looked different to the one that West Germany won in 1954. The 1958 version appeared to be 5cm taller and had a different base.

MYSTERY: Was the 1958 trophy a copy? If so, where is the original?
STATUS: UNSOLVED

Mystery 2: Stolen on a Sunday

In 1966, England hosted the World Cup. The Jules Rimet trophy was on display in a central London museum for a few months before the tournament began. One Sunday, when the guards were not looking, a thief or thieves broke in through the back doors and stole the trophy. It was a huge embarrassment for English football and Scotland Yard was called in to solve the crime.

MYSTERY: Where was the trophy?
STATUS: A dog called Pickles found it seven days later, wrapped in newspaper under a bush in South London.

MYSTERY: Who was behind the theft?
STATUS:

Mystery 3: Burglary in Brazil

FIFA had a rule that the first country to win the World Cup three times would be allowed to keep the trophy. When Brazil won their third title in 1970, the Brazilians took the Jules Rimet trophy home. In 1983, it was stolen from the third floor of the Brazilian Football Confederation office in Rio de Janeiro. No one has seen it since. Brazil's investigators said it had been melted down into gold bars, but this can't be right, since the original trophy wasn't made of gold!

MYSTERY: Where is the trophy?
STATUS:

After 1970, FIFA had a new trophy made. This time it was made of gold and featured two human figures holding up a globe. So far this trophy hasn't gone missing. In fact, Ben once visited FIFA HQ in Zurich and is one of the few Englishmen to have lifted it!

Whoever gets to the bottom of either of the three unsolved mysteries above would be a true world champion, a soccer Sherlock Holmes.

If you have any ideas, please let us know!

CUP CALAMITIES

Defender Sergio Ramos dropped the Copa del Rey, or King's Cup, in 2011 when Real Madrid were parading through the city in an open-topped bus. The bus ran the cup over and squashed it. Ooops!

Fireworks and confetti were released as Brazilian team Corinthians lifted the trophy after winning the 2009 local championship. The paper and fireworks landed in the trophy, which caught fire. Hot stuff!

The world's smallest football trophy is just 6 millimetres high. It is given to the winners of the Lyonesse Cup, an annual match between the Isles of Scilly, which are just off Cornwall, and Dynamo Choughs, from Penzance. Not big but very Scilly!

DESIGN AND TECHNOLOGY QUIZ

1. What was the prize for victorious athletes in the first Olympic games?

a) A lifetime supply of olive oil
b) A crown of olive leaves
c) Shampoo made out of olive juice
d) A golden olive

2. What surprise was in store for Sunderland's players after they lost the 1992 FA Cup final to Liverpool?

a) They found the FA Cup trophy on their coach home.
b) They were all presented with winners' medals by mistake.
c) The FA couldn't find the trophy so asked both teams to replay the match.
d) They travelled back to Sunderland in a hot air balloon in the shape of the FA Cup trophy.

3. In France, the Champions League trophy is known as La Coupe aux Grandes Oreilles. What does that mean?

a) The Cup of Great Drama
b) The Cup that Never Ends
c) The Cup with Big Ears
d) The Cup of Oreo Cookies

4. What are the chemical symbols for gold and silver?

a) Au and Ag
b) Go and Si
c) Bling and Sparkle
d) ¥ and $

5. What was the name of the film that starred Pickles the dog, who found fame after his World Cup discovery?

a) The Spy with the Cold Nose
b) The Detective with Long Ears
c) The Sleuth and his Pooch
d) The Dog Who Loved Me

Congratulations! You've reached the end of the book.
You deserve a trophy!
In fact, we have one for you ... it's blue on the outside, made from a tree, rectangular in shape and has 176 pages!
Can you guess what it is? Raise it above your head and hear our applause. Hooray!
You're a champion of knowledge because you now know:
Why feet are so pongy!
How high an Ethiopian wild goat can jump.
Your chances of winning a coin toss.
And what steel has got to do with the beginning of football.
AB
BL

We've met the animal that only dozes for two hours a day.
The tallest – and shortest – teams in the world.
You can now commentate as if you are from Braziiiiiiiiiiiillll!
And dress like a fashion icon!
Well, apart from you, Ben!
Stop it! Your jokes are bad for my health.
Your elf? Have you been to Iceland again? You need to chill out!
And so do you! Time for a break I think...
See you back here for Football School Season 4!
We can't wait!
AB
BL

QUIZ ANSWERS

BIOLOGY
1. a
2. c
3. b
4. d
5. c

ENGLISH
1. b
2. c
3. c
4. a
5. a

PHYSICS
1. a
2. c
3. b
4. d
5. a

ZOOLOGY
1. d
2. a
3. a
4. b
5. d

POLITICS
1. b
2. c
3. c
4. a
5. a

PSHE
1. c
2. b
3. c
4. d
5. c

SCHOOL TRIP
1. d
2. a
3. d
4. c
5. a

HISTORY
1. c
2. b
3. b
4. c
5. a

MATHS
1. b
2. a
3. c
4. b
5. d

GEOGRAPHY
1. c
2. b
3. d
4. b
5. b

CHEMISTRY
1. d
2. c
3. b
4. a
5. b

FASHION
1. d
2. a
3. b
4. d
5. c

DESIGN AND TECHNOLOGY
1. b
2. b
3. c
4. a
5. a

ACKNOWLEDGEMENTS

We know that TEAM stands for Together Everyone Achieves More and we are lucky to have the best team in the world at Football School. Once again, our illustrator Spike Gerrell has played a blinder. He wins the Football School Golden Crayon - thank you, Spike!

The backroom team at Walker have coached us to perfection. Head coach Daisy Jellicoe has led from the front, with great support from sporting director Denise Johnstone-Burt and Louise Jackson, Laurelie Bazin, Megan Middleton, Rosi Crawley, John Moore, Jill Kidson, James McParland, Ed Ripley and Jo Humphreys-Davies.

We have loved working with our publicist Jo Hardacre and social media stars Naomi Bacon and Marion Honey.

Thanks to our agents Rebecca Carter, Rebecca Folland, Kirsty Gordon, David Luxton, Rebecca Winfield and Nick Waters for keeping us fired up and focussed.

We would also like to thank the following experts for sharing their time and knowledge with us: Simon Austin, Tony Barrett, Federico Bassahun, Michael Beale, Max Boon, Dr Tony Collins, Dermot Corrigan, Andy Dixon, Reg Elliot, Dr Luke Ettinger, Dr Majid Ezzati, Tom Fattorini, Margaret Fern, Sarah Galgey, Ken Gibb, Serafino Ingardia, Hans Leitert, Nick Littlehales, Professor Stuart Lyon, Richard McBrearty, David McParland, Dr Carmen Mangion, David Moor at www.historicalkits.co.uk, Matt Rapinet, Darren Rodman at Pitchmark Ltd, Nutan Shah and Ron McCulloch of the London Podiatry Centre, Luke Shiach, Dr Stasinos Stavrianeas and Adam Witchell.

Shout out to our Star Pupils: Samuel Clegg, Ayalah Honigstein, Finn Inglethorpe, Matti Wilkins Strelitz and Tami Wilkins Strelitz. And from Arnot St Mary Primary School, Liverpool: Tamasin Robinson, Tom Kelly and Emily Heavyside. From Knowsley Central School, Liverpool: Ava Dooley, Alfie Whittick, Ruby Wood, Todd Smith, Thomas Gibbons and Tom Mather.

Ben would like to thank Annie for her continuing inspiration and support, and Clemmy and Bibi for adding the best jokes in here and cheering on Football School across the country.

Alex would like to thank Natalie for cheering from the terraces, and Barnaby and Zak for keeping the volume up.

ABOUT YOUR COACHES

Alex Bellos writes for the *Guardian* and has written several bestselling popular science books.

Ben Lyttleton is an author, broadcaster and consultant to professional football clubs.

Spike Gerrell draws cartoons for magazines and books.

Coming soon

Coming soon